The Ghosts of Mérida

Thrilling Accounts of Souls, Spirits, and Ghosts of Mexico's Most Haunted City

Louis E.V. Nevaer

The Ghosts
of Mérida

Thrilling Accounts
of Souls, Spirits, and Ghosts
of Mexico's Most Haunted City

Louis E.V. Nevaer

ATTENTION CORPORATIONS, UNIVERSITIES, COLLEGES,
AND PROFESSIONAL AND CHARITABLE
ORGANIZATIONS: Quantity discounts are available on bulk
purchases of this book for educational and gift purposes, or as
premiums in fundraising efforts. Inquiries should be sent to
info@hispaniceconomics.com.

Hispanic Economics, Inc.
P.O. Box 140681
Coral Gables, FL 33114-0681
info@hispaniceconomics.com
HispanicEconomics.com

ISBN 978-0-9791176-8-8

Cover, photo montages, and interior design by John Clifton
john@johnclifton.net

For Joann Andrews

A spirited presence in Mérida if ever there was one

Table of Contents

✠ Preface ✠

érida was founded on January 6, 1542. It is one of the oldest cities founded by Europeans in the New World.

It is therefore not surprising that a city of this age is home to many bewitched buildings and resident ghosts. If one considers that Mérida was founded on the ruins of the abandoned Maya ceremonial center of T-hó, the possibilities for paranormal activity increase.

When this project to assemble the ghost stories of Mérida began, there were a handful of ghost sightings identified. There are now more than 320. This book is a compilation of 36 of the more interesting—and *verified*—reports of ghosts, spirits, and souls. In addition, thirty-six other cases of haunted residences are under final review. It should be noted that the book concludes with a brief discussion of the two confirmed sightings of the Virgin of Guadalupe.

Believer or doubter, it matters not. These stories are intended to help readers become more aware of their own sixth sense.

What was that noise? Who is that figure in the distance? Do you hear that music? Who's singing that song? Did you just feel something?

What if? What if it is true?

Open your mind to the possibility that the being making that noise, or the apparition in the distance, or the source of that music, or the creature singing that melody could possibly be . . . *metaphysical.*

It will make you a better person.
I invite you to enjoy these tiny tales of terror.

Louis E. V. Nevaer
Mérida, Yucatán

෨❉෨

✠ Introduction ✠

hen the building that houses Casa Catherwood was purchased in 2006 for the purpose of providing a permanent exhibition of the lithographs created by Englishman Frederick Catherwood in the nineteenth century, it took ten months of design and reconstruction to restore it.

After the work was completed, the family from which the house was purchased returned for a private tour. They brought an old album filled with photographs of the original family that lived here from the 1900s to the 1950s. I looked through the photos and familiarized myself with the family members.

Then the matriarch casually commented, "A ghost lives here and next door. Have you heard her yet?"

So began an informal interest in the haunted houses of Mérida and ghost stories. This query was emboldened by Emilio Chan, a Maya healer who is a member of the Organization of Indigenous Maya Herbalists of the Yucatán Peninsula, or OMIMPY, and is recognized as a spiritual leader of the Maya people. He confirmed the presence of spirits in this building, and the adjacent one as well. Alejandro Caamal, a master mason and contractor, who has worked in hundreds of houses in town over the years, reported encountering ghosts on many occasions. His workers have also reported seeing ghosts at many sites.

This book is a collection of some of the more fascinating ghost stories investigated to date. What is astounding is the energy that certain places appear to have. For example, if in the course of investigating a haunting it was learned that a suicide took place in the 1830s in a specific house, then decades later, when the house was sold to another family, it might turn out that a suicide took place in that new family. Does this mean that the building drives people to suicide? Or that people who are inclined to commit suicide are drawn to that place?

These are questions that lend themselves to the contemplation of life, fate—and the afterlife.

Enjoy the stories collected here. There will be more as our investigations into paranormal activity continue.

Alberto Huchim

Manager, Casa Catherwood
Mérida, Yucatán

The Ghosts of the Historic Centro

The Soul of the ✠ Sacrificial Maya ✠ Virgin

There is no doubt that, for centuries, people have heard the voice of a woman along Calle 60 in downtown Mérida, just a block north of the cathedral.

Those who claim to be reasonable, sensible people have been dismissive of any and all accounts of hearing the voice, attributing them to the overactive imaginations or wishful thinking of hysterics.

Yet women in particular consistently report hearing the soft voice of a female near Parque Hidalgo, which boasts an elaborate statue of the infamous nineteenth-century hero General Manuel Cepeda. This park featured prominently in Francisco Montejo's original plan for the city.

Documentation of witnesses—again, primarily women—who hear a female reciting indiscernible orations

1

dates back to the 1840s. This haunting offers an explanation for the absence of residences in the area: No one wanted to live in a neighborhood where the voice of a woman reciting incantations was heard as the sun went down.

The Maya attributed the noises and disturbances to the *Aloxob*—trickster sprites or spirits they believe are mischievous. These creatures are said to live in caves, under stones, or in cornfields and are said to taunt humans with their pranks. The Spaniards considered an *alux* to be a *duende*, roughly analogous to the goblins, faeries, or leprechauns of European traditions, and dismissed them as imaginary creatures. ("Alux" is singular, and "aloxob" is plural.)

The voice continued to be heard across the centuries. What made it more intriguing was that most Europeans could not make out the words. We now know the reason: The soul was speaking in an ancient dialect of Yucatec Maya.

This was not an evening or a nighttime haunting, a simple observation that in itself offered clues. It was not the place of the tormented.

In our time, the voice is often described as being melodious, seductive, and enchanting, qualities that have led observers to believe that, if anything, the voice is that of a kind of siren, elusive and irresistible. In the European tradition, however, sirens are dangerous creatures, seductresses who lead men to their doom.

Here, in Yucatán, it is not clear if there is malice associated with this spot. At dusk, the incessant sound of birds gathering to nest for the night is said to drown out the soul's voice. Some claim the birds make a ruckus for the expressed purpose of protecting the living from the woman whose voice is heard.

What is one to make sense of this presence?

Spiritualists have long rejected the impulse to compare Maya beliefs to European traditions. An *alux* as a goblin? A Maya soul as a siren?

The suggestions continue, however. Among the more exceptional witnesses is none other than Katharine Hepburn, who stayed at the Hotel Itzá, a block from this park, when she was in Mérida in May 1939. (The hotel today is a school.) In her journal Miss Hepburn reported hearing a melody coming from a young woman "reciting neither Spanish, nor English" in the "vicinity of the Park where we strolled through enjoying ice cones." She concluded it must have been a "Maya faerie."

In the 1950s several purification ceremonies were held in the park. The hope was to grant this soul permission to depart this world. One shaman claimed to have made contact with the young woman. She told him she was careworn from her limbo of immortality. He reported that she communicated to him that she had been a virgin sacrificed in what corresponds to 584 C.E. in our calendar. This account being published in 2012, that would place her death approximately 1,428 years ago.

Could there be any truth to this claim? Is it possible that the soul of a Maya virgin sacrificed to Chaac, the rain god, is still lingering in T-hó, the pre-Hispanic name for Mérida?

What is one to make of the idea that a Maya maiden has stood guardian over this place for more than fourteen centuries?

It is, of course, easy to dismiss these claims as ridiculous. Most people have.

That is, until December 2011.

That was when municipal workers stumbled upon a burial site that predates the arrival of the Spanish by several hundred years. Human remains were found deep within the earth beneath the park. Until then, no one knew that this was the location of an ancient Maya burial site.

Had they uncovered the human remains of the Maya Sacrificial Virgin whose voice has been heard in this park for centuries? Had they found physical evidence of this soul?

Who can answer with certainty?

After all, in the hundreds of years that Europeans have lived here, no one knew that only a city block north of the cathedral lay an important Maya burial site.

The discovery of these human remains made front-page news throughout México when it was revealed to the public. All work was suspended to allow archaeologists to excavate and investigate this burial site. Even the most skeptical of observers were presented with undeniable proof: Human bones were buried beneath the very spot where the seductive incantations of a Maya maiden have called out to the living for hundreds of years.

Since then, spiritualists from the world over have converged here in various efforts to establish a rapport with the soul that inhabits this place.

No one has established contact with her. What is known is that the Soul of the Sacrificial Virgin has fallen silent since the burial site was uncovered.

Has she been released from this place? Has she chosen to remain silent? Has the desecration of her resting place changed the dynamics of her existence?

These are questions that can only be answered with time, if at all. For now, the familiar voice in the park at dusk remains elusive.

Spiritualists differ on what has occurred.

Will she speak again? Will she reveal her name?

Will you be present to hear her melodious voice rise above the sound of the birds as they assemble at dusk for the night?

Paranormal Activity: Soul

Address: Hidalgo Park, corner of Calle 60 and 59th Street, Centro

Classification: Benevolent

The Mother-Daughter ✠ Concerto ✠

By any standard, the once gracious home on Calle 56, number 483, between Calle 55 and 57 Street, speaks of a history of wealth and privilege.

It reflects the sensibilities of the late Victorian and Edwardian eras, when Mérida enjoyed a resurgence in bold architecture and an exciting transformation of the city's look. Hundreds of two-story mansions were built.

This gracious residence was one of the new buildings raised to the demanding standards of Mérida's elite. Their insistence on excellence extended at times to how the owners lived their own lives.

For more than eighty years passersby have reported hearing voices and music coming from this building. They hear the soft exchange between a mother and her daughter. Their conversation, almost inaudible, revolves around the need for discipline and practice. The mother insists, "One more time. From the beginning."

Then the music is heard.

Faint but distinct, it is heard in late evening, but there are no reports of it being heard after 11 P.M. Many think that the spirit of the daughter, who is believed to be no older than fourteen, went to sleep at that hour. Attempts to record the voices and music have been unsuccessful.

The haunting and music is so frequent, however, that the melody has been identified by two musical authorities: Violin Concerto in B minor, op. 61, by Edward Elgar.

This long orchestral composition, first performed in London in 1910, has enthralled generations of music lovers around the world. In Mérida, playing this violin concerto was seen as a cultural manifestation in support of the Allies during the Great War, more commonly known as World War I.

Little is known about the political views of this mother-daughter pair of music aficionados. The spirits discuss discipline and practice but not politics.

If in the late evening you should think you are hearing what resembles Edward Elgar's violin concerto near this house, remember: She has been practicing for more than a century.

And remember one other thing: The music is not being played by the living.

Paranormal Activity: **Spirits**

Address: **Calle 56 #483, between Calle 55 and 57 Street, Centro**

Classification: **Benign**

The Ghost of the Betrayed Soldier

✠ ✠

I t is the ghost of a lost soul, the ghost of a soldier who returned home from the devastating War of the Castes to find his family dead. It is the ghost of a man so disoriented by his grief that he could not bear the consequences of a war, dated 1847 to 1901, that represents half a century of civil unrest in Yucatán.

The story begins with this unnecessary war. It ends with grief so unbearable that this soldier hanged himself from the rafters of the Templo de la Mejorada.

Built in 1640, as a Franciscan monastery, this vast church and convent is located on the corner of Calle 59 and Calle 50.

The ghost is seen wandering, a solitary figure, along the Templo and former Convent of the Mejorada. In life he was a forlorn man, one the parish priest described as suffering from a "mind possessed by divine madness" and an "incurable" melancholy.

"The truth is not kind," the priest counseled when trying to explain the loss of his family. "This is the nature of our fleeting journey through this world. What matters is how we conduct ourselves, and how we prepare for our eternal reward."

The soldier was unconvinced.

"Nothing is colder than a heart closing shut," the soldier replied. "A man's hearing is never more acute than when it is told lies."

The priest was taken aback. Who would dare speak this way?

In the nineteenth century, Stoicism influenced the attitudes of people in Yucatán as they confronted the ravages of civil war. Towns and villages had been decimated by bloodshed. The upheaval was intensified by the slaughter of entire families, resulting in the collapse of entire communities.

Many of the ruined haciendas that litter Yucatán are the direct result of the War of the Castes. Residents fled and never returned. In some cases, all the inhabitants of isolated haciendas were massacred at once.

"This is the way of the world," the priest offered as solace to the soldier who returned from war to find his wife and children had been killed. They had been sent to a town thought to be safe, only to find death at the hands—and machetes—of rebel Maya.

Then, as now, the afternoon air hung soft, fragrant with blossoms. Birds flew from tree to tree. The sun moved across the sky. Life went on; life always goes on.

"The air is soft and pleasing," the soldier said. "It speaks of everything." But it was little consolation.

In nineteenth-century Yucatán, men returning from the War of the Castes to devastated lives were offered the consolation of philosophy. The Archdiocese in Yucatan availed itself of the Greek classics to help men understand and cope with the madness around them. Ajax, a play written by Sophocles in the fifth century B.C.E., explored the nature of warriors returning from the battlefield. Sophocles himself was a general and a war veteran. Ajax takes place after the Iliad but before the conclusion of the Trojan War.

The theme of the play is how Ajax comes to terms with the fluid nature of life, a world that is in a constant flux. "All I want is to feel the same, for life to be the same, to go back to how my life was before war interrupted it," Ajax implies in the unraveling of his mind.

But the world is ever changing; nothing is permanent. "Escape from heaven-sent madness is none," the chorus sings in Ajax.

Priests sought to help veterans and survivors rebuild their lives and recover from devastating loss. They offered comforting platitudes. As the years of warfare and the number of dead mounted, their words proved less effective.

Was it possible to offer comfort to people who were living through senseless death all around them? Was there any point to this endless war?

"O Death, Death, come now and look upon me," Ajax pleads moments before committing suicide.

In the camaraderie of soldiers across the ages, the young soldier from Mérida who found life unbearable without his wife and children took his own life. He hung himself inside the church, his body suspended and swaying softly in the afternoon air so fragrant with blossoms.

His ghost, that of a man betrayed by the false honor of war, wanders Mejorada Park in the cool of late afternoons. He walks in silence, without purpose.

Do you feel his presence?

Do you understand why hearing is most acute when one is told lies?

Do you sense the futility of endless wars that result in a numbing drumbeat of casualties? Is it possible to live in a society where war is without end and remain sane?

Is it any wonder the air is so soft in Mejorada Park? Is it any wonder that it speaks of everything?

In his silence, the ghost of the soldier betrayed by war also speaks everything.

Paranormal Activity: **Ghost**

Address: **Mejorada Church, corner of Calle 59 and 50th Street, Centro**

Classification: **Benign**

The Drums of the Anguished Slaves

✠ ✠

The Church of Santa Lucia is a historic structure. Only a few blocks north of the massive cathedral, its very modesty may be seen as remarkable.

Santa Lucia sits in a lovely shaded courtyard in the city's historic Centro. It's quite possible to walk by and hardly notice it.

That was the intention. Constructed away from the street, the church was not intended to be immediately visible to the casual passerby, whether a pedestrian or in a horse-drawn carriage.

Santa Lucia, after all, was the neighborhood designated for mulattoes and blacks to live and worship. For decades blacks outnumbered whites in Mérida. Many of them were brought here in bondage. This reflected the harsh realities of the conflict between church and state. The Franciscan missionaries claimed jurisdiction over the Maya and forbade civil authorities from conscripting them for forced labor. Civil authorities, confronting a labor shortage, responded by importing blacks and mulattoes from Cuba and other Caribbean islands.

Santa Lucia thus became the parish church for those society held in lowest esteem: slaves and mixed-raced residents. It is revealing that, in 1804, when the governor of the state, General Benito Pérez Valdelomar, initiated the construction of the plaza that faces the Church of Santa Lucia, he declared: "Wanting to beautify the capital every day more, I've dedicated myself to transforming into a

colorful and pleasant plaza the foul and disgusting pigsty of Santa Lucia."

As part of the renovations, the cemetery that stood between the sidewalk and the church was demolished.

Indeed, the shaded terrace one sees today was the first burial ground for the city's population of slaves and mixed-race residents. As such, it also represents the legacy of Africans torn from their homelands and shipped to the New World beginning in the 1670s, when the British controlled the Slave Castle of Cape Coast, the point of embarkation for those sent to their destinies in the Americas. From that port, slaves arrived in the Caribbean, and from there they were sold to masters throughout New Spain.

In Mérida, slaves and mulattoes were relegated to the area adjoining Santa Lucia and were forbidden to enter the cathedral in the main square. Their spiritual needs were attended to by the priests who conducted services at Santa Lucia. Under the priests' auspices, blacks and mulattoes were permitted to tend to the cemetery.

When Governor Pérez Valdelomar began his renovation of Santa Lucia, there was much turmoil. The longtime residents of the neighborhood resented and resisted being ordered to relocate to other areas of the city. Some stood to lose their homes, a dislocation that resulted in much confusion, since the disenfranchised residents of Santa Lucia did not have the economic wherewithal to find accommodations they would have liked, and thus established living arrangements were broken. Many were forced to endure long commutes to attend Mass at Santa Lucia. Others met resistance in the form of discrimination in other neighborhoods whose residents did not welcome blacks or mulattoes living near them.

Fearing an uprising, Governor Pérez Valdelomar made it clear that any civil disorder would be met with a ban on the public playing of drums. One of the few cultural expressions permitted in the neighborhood of Santa Lucia was the playing of African drums and the singing of African songs. It was not uncommon for the melodies of western Africa to waft through the area's streets in the evenings. It was said that the soothing melodies of Africa and the soft murmur of African drums mingled in the air for all to enjoy.

One man from Santa Lucia stepped forward as a liaison to encourage a dialogue between the community and the authorities about this ambitious renovation. He emerged as the one person who could smooth things between the residents of Santa Lucia and the governor. This peacekeeper is remembered by his baptismal name, Martín Bonaficio. Although he had been brought to Mérida in bondage, he had been granted freedom and lived as a free man respected by slaves, free blacks, mulattoes, and the white elite.

It was out of benevolence that Martín Bonafacio endeavored to reconcile the discontent the black and mulatto residents felt. He reminded them that at times in life one's fate is not in one's hands, and he achieved a general resignation to the governor's undertaking. The only outcries against the governor arose when the cemetery was cleared away. As it was never explained why the dead had to be moved or where their remains were taken, this was seen as an act of desecration.

Drums beat in protest, and several groups of blacks engaged in African practices, almost resembling what would become Santería—combining Catholic symbols with African rituals—to make amends for the sins Mérida's officials were committing against the community's dead. West African drums sounded in anger, and songs were sung to repent for the desecration.

It is said that blood saturated the ground around the Church of Santa Lucia, which is why it remains a rust color today. It is said that when the Church of Santa Lucia was painted white, blood flowed from the stone walls, and that is why the church is painted pink. Martín Bonafacio promised that the drums of Africa would forevermore be heard in Santa Lucia, and that he would stand guard, as a presence, to ensure it would be so.

The promise Martín Bonafacio made is said to endure. During the hot summer months, when the city is all but deserted, one can hear the soft echoes of distant drums.

Many claim that it is the souls of the anguished slaves who, in defiance, play their drums to drown out Governor Pérez Valdelomar's cries from Hell. There are continuing reports of low-pitched sounds and rhythms wafting through the streets in late summer afternoons. Some claim to see the ghost of Martín Bonafacio tending the grounds around the Church, sweeping the leaves that now fall on the cobblestones that cover the former graves of long-dead slaves.

Who can say?

What can be said with confidence is that this is the story of a man who, born free in Africa, enslaved by the British, and held in bondage by the Spaniards, died a free man in Mérida. This is a melancholy haunting, the presence of a good man who watches over Santa Lucia against the backdrop of the sounds of west Africa.

If you glimpse the apparition of a black man in the courtyard or hear the soft and distant sounds of drums, consider yourself fortunate.

This is what life is all about it, isn't it—the legacy that unites us all across the ages? The beat of distant drums is not unlike the beat of your mother's heart, the rhythm of life that gave you life.

It is that beautiful.

Paranormal Activity: Spirit

Address: Santa Lucia Church, corner of Calle 60 and 55th Street, Centro

Classification: Benevolent

✠ The Disembodied Head ✠

I t's a creation myth. It's a recent apparition, one said to be associated with 2012. It's a sight to behold, housed in a building that dates back to 1727.

We are speaking about the tree in the patio of Alberto's Continental Cuisine, located on the corner of Calle 57 and Calle 64 in the heart of the historic Centro. This is a restaurant run by two Lebanese brothers, Alberto and Pedro, whose family fled turmoil in the Middle East and found refuge and peace in Yucatán.

The patio in this historic building, graced by *mudejar*-patterned tiles and Moorish arches, is noted for memorable drinks and fine meals. Yes, it's been a stellar restaurant since the 1970s, and today it offers romantic elegance. Many fine memories of visits to Mérida are made here.

The establishment has one more thing going for it: In its courtyard there's a massive rubber tree.

In Maya mythology Xquic, a lovely Maya maiden, gave birth to Hunahpu and Xbalanque, who became the Hero Twins and saved their people. Legend has it that the disembodied head of their father, also named Hunahpu, was hung from a gourd in a tree after he had been defeated in a ball game by the Lords of the Underworld. Xquic approached the tree, against her family's wishes, and Hunahpu spoke to her. He asked her to extend her hand. She did. He spat into her palm. In that moment, she became pregnant with the twin boys.

A familiar story, isn't it? A maiden. An immaculate conception. The birth of saviors.

What is one to make of this?

More important, what is one to make of reports that the head of Hunahpu has been spotted in this rubber tree, in this patio, in this city?

"I'm most happy when the night has gone black," he is reported as saying. "I will bear the misery of the world if it were to pour down on me from the heavens! I will take the world's misery!"

One psychic, Carmen Zúñiga, claims to have communicated with him. She reports he is here to reassure the world. She claims that as the current cycle ends during the winter solstice 2012 and another begins the following day, he has appeared to guide humanity into the new cycle.

He is appearing now to reassure humanity that the world—life—will continue.

Is it possible?

Is the disembodied head of Hunahpu, father of the Hero Twins, in Mérida?

Is he here to assure us that the world will continue beyond 2012?

Paranormal Activity: **Ghost**

Address: **Alberto's Continental, corner of Calle 57 and 64th Street, Centro**

Classification: **Benevolent**

The Christian Martyr ✠ of Mérida ✠

hat is known about this soul is that he is not at rest. What is also not in dispute is that he is the oldest known ghost of a European to inhabit Mérida. His name is lost to history, but the circumstances surrounding this death—and the reason for his haunting—are well established.

To understand the nature of his haunting, it is first necessary to understand his life.

He was a soldier, a poor Spaniard who arrived in the New World with hopes of making a name, a life, and a fortune for himself. He envisioned wealth and success, and he dreamt of then returning to Spain to find a wife and live in comfort. He saw a future in which he fathered children and would enjoy the privilege of seeing them become successful men and women.

His was the familiar expectation of the hundreds of Spanish adventurers who sailed from Spain to Yucatán. Often from poor, rural families, they imagined that untold wealth could be theirs, along with the promise of a prompt return to the world they knew: Spain.

What this poor soldier found was a different destiny, one that he resisted at first—and then embraced for the sake of his faith.

He arrived in Yucatán by choice. He was under the command of Alonso López, who was ordered by Francisco

"El Mozo" Montejo to conquer the Maya areas south of Mérida. This took place a few years after the founding of Mérida in 1542. The military objective was to establish Spanish jurisdiction among the Maya communities to the south. It was a time of great social transition: Maya and Spaniard found themselves both living among the ruins of the collapsed classic Maya civilization.

At its apogee this civilization had a population numbered in the millions. The Maya, by the sixteenth century, had been reduced to a few tens of thousands of souls living in scattered communities throughout the peninsula. Gone were their kings, their priests, their teachers. They had lost the ability to read and write. Their histories were little more than oral traditions. When the Spanish arrived and asked who had built their temples, the Maya said they did not know. When the Spanish asked who could read the inscriptions on the pyramids, no one could. When the Spanish inquired about the one central authority, there was none.

Amid the disparate Maya communities, there was disagreement about what to make of the Spanish. There was something odd about a people who were intent on building massive structures and laying out formal cities. What was their obsession with reading and with writing things down? Who was this king of theirs who lived in a place so distant he never visited them? Who was this mysterious God of theirs who was always spoken about with reverence but who, again, was never seen?

Some Maya communities welcomed the Spaniards. The Spanish did bring all manner of desirable goods, from oranges to pigs, horses to metal tools. Other Maya communities were indifferent: The world was a big enough place for everyone. A good number of Maya communities, on the other hand, resisted these interlopers, especially the way they wished to impose their faith and language on them.

There was nothing wrong with their religious practices, many Maya communities believed, even if their own priests were unable to read the sacred texts of their ancestors. Then again, there was something appealing about Christianity: The idea of nailing someone to a cross and watching him die seemed, on many levels, a fun show to watch. The Maya, after all, were experts when it came to human sacrifice and worshipping gods who required the flow of human blood.

Christians, in other words, had little to teach the Maya about sadism.

It was against this background that Alonso López was ordered to move south and extend the jurisdiction of the Spanish. It was, by all accounts, a dangerous mission.

The Maya communities to the south resisted the Spanish and wanted nothing to do with them. They had learned enough about Christianity to be indifferent to it. They resisted the idea that they would have to abandon their own religious beliefs and practices. They were determined to fight the Spanish and the imposition of a foreign way of life.

Who wants to settle for the metaphor of human sacrifice on a cross when one can indulge in real human sacrifice?

It was no surprise, then, that Alonso López and his men were seized upon by the Maya near present-day Tekax. It was to be expected that some of the Spanish would become separated from their countrymen as they retreated. It was not without consequence that a few of the men were captured by the Maya.

Among them was this humble soldier who was destined never to return to his homeland.

What is known is that it would take almost a decade before the Maya from this area of the peninsula were subjugated, at least in theory. Relations between Spaniard and Maya were peaceful enough to allow for the office of the Commissioner General of New Spain to visit Tekax in 1558.

What is also known is that, near the cathedral on the Zócalo in downtown Mérida, reports of the apparition of a ghost surface each August. He wanders near the entrance of the cathedral, occasionally walking across the street and back.

In centuries past, he was said to tell his tale, at times in words but more often by possessing the thoughts of witnesses.

He claims that he fell behind as Alonso López and his companions retreated to safety. He tells of being captured by the Maya. He laments being held captive for weeks, until the day came when he knew he would be slain.

He tells that a Maya priest from a different village arrived with an entourage. The men held Christian books in their hands. He tells of them pointing to an image in the book and pointing to him. He recalls being stripped naked, then tied to a wooden cross, and, with blades, he was flayed alive.

The doomed man recalls the horror of having his skin cut away in strips and how he cried out to Saint Bartholomew, who was flayed in the first century. The ghost claims the last thought he had while alive in this world was that he welcomed this death if his martyrdom would ensure that Christianity would prevail over this land.

The Christian Martyr of Mérida is easy to identify: His ghost is that of a man who has no skin and whose muscles are visible. Witnesses swear that, at times, he is clothed in rags, but as he approaches, they realize these are remnants of skin that hang from his mutilated body.

The last documentation attesting to this ghost's words being relayed to the living dates to 1809. It is in the form of an entry in the journal of a visitor who recorded her encounter with the ghost telling her of his martyrdom. Since that time, he has appeared consistently, but he has not communicated with the living. It is said that he utters, on occasion, one sentence, but as if speaking to himself: "It is an honor to have died in the manner of Saint Bartholomew."

He most frequently appears on August 24, the feast day of Saint Bartholomew, according to reports. It is said that he is visible when the bells toll in the afternoon, calling the faithful to assemble and celebrate their Christian faith.

Some claim he stands guardian over Christianity in Yucatán.

Paranormal Activity: **Soul**

Address: **Cathedral, Zócalo, corner of Calle 60 and 61st Street, Centro**

Classification: **Benevolent**

The Souls of the
✠ House of the ✠
Inquisition

O n the corner of Calle 61 and Calle 66 one finds a property abandoned, locked up, and in complete shambles.

Legend has it that in this place those condemned to be interviewed by the authorities of the Inquisition waited for their appointments.

It was the sixteenth century, when people believed that Satan intervened actively in human affairs. People feared sorcerers and looked to the angels and the saints for relief. At this time strict rules governed how people lived their lives and worked to save their souls.

In Yucatán a great debate arose from one philosophical question: Were the Maya subject to religious jurisdiction?

The question pitted two Franciscans against each other. Bishop Francisco de Toral, the first bishop of Yucatán (1561–1571), believed the Maya had fully to understand Christianity before they could be subject to Church discipline. Diego de Landa, who succeeded him as bishop in October 1572, believed that, once baptized, the Maya were subject to the jurisdiction of the Catholic faith.

The souls that mourn in this place—the so-called House of the Inquisition's office—offer evidence of the vexing nature of this philosophical conflict. The haunting screams heard in the night echo down the centuries. Muffled cries

and supplications to a distant God are heard by the living to this day.

The differences of opinion between Toral and Landa resulted in scandal. Toral feared what would happen once he passed from this life; he suspected that Landa was of unstable mind. "Our brother Landa is misguided in some of his beliefs," Toral complained to ecclesiastical authorities at the Council of the Indies in Madrid. Toral's fears were not without merit. As bishop, Landa launched a series of autos-da-fé in the town of Maní that became infamous.

Landa had become convinced that the fallen angel Lucifer—Satan himself—had arrived in Yucatán. He established an Inquisition to determine if the Maya had been led astray by Satan and had returned to engage in pagan rituals, including human sacrifice.

In short order, civic authorities were involved; the Inquisition was wreaking havoc and fomenting rebellion against Spanish authority throughout Yucatán.

Landa was accused of establishing an Inquisition without authorization and of conducting illegal autos-da-fé. The question of whether the recent Maya converts were subject to the Church's laws had not been answered in a definite manner. He was accused before the Council of the Indies of violating church law. Landa was summoned to Spain and ordered to explain himself before authorities in Madrid. The proceedings before the Council of the Indies opened an intellectual and philosophical line of inquiry that reshaped the nature of belief and discipline.

Within the context of the time, it must be remembered, the only proper response to accusations made against someone in the course of a religious proceeding was silence.

The reason was convoluted: If one confessed, the confession was admission of guilt. If one professed innocence and there was a single witness to contradict that claim, then one was guilty of deception. If one refused to answer, then it was evidence that the Holy Ghost had interceded on one's behalf.

Refusal to answer was the only reasonable course of action. It would then be up to church authorities to debate among themselves the merits of the accusations and the evidence brought before them.

In what would become the United States, the most compelling example of this Christian juridical procedure occurred in Salem, Massachusetts. In Arthur Miller's The

Crucible, Giles Corey is accused of witchcraft. The historical Corey was subjected to judicial torture by the authorities in April 1692. He refused to answer one way or the other. He was then pressed with heavy stones until he was crushed to death. In the play, Elizabeth Proctor describes the scene this way:

He were not hanged. He would not answer yes or no to his indictment; for if he denied the charge they'd hang him surely, and auction out his property. So he stand mute, and died Christian under the law. And so his sons will have his farm. It is the law, for he could not be condemned a wizard without he answer the indictment, aye or nay.

More than a century before, Landa subjected scores of Maya converts to Christianity to an Inquisition.

The contemporary view is that Landa became possessed by Satan himself or that he grew delirious and suffered a psychotic episode. His establishment of an Inquisition was a source of furious debate and controversy. When Yucatán governor Francisco Velázquez de Gijón ordered an end to Landa's activities, Landa retaliated by accusing the governor of being in consort with Satan and excommunicating him.

After Landa was replaced as Bishop of Yucatán in 1577 and ordered back to Spain he had time to reflect on the decisions he had taken. He was summoned to explain his actions in Yucatán before the Council of the Indies and was described as having gone mad.

More than four centuries later, should you stand on this corner it is still possible to hear the pleadings of the Maya converts who waited their turn to answer before the Inquisition. Some claim they hear the phrase, "This is the part of me that is eternal." Others report hearing: "My soul is sacrosanct." Another common variation: "No one can seize my eternal soul, which belongs to Christ."

What these souls do not understand is that the only proper reply is silence. Those accused before the Inquisition must avail themselves of the Silence of the Holy Ghost if they hope to be absolved.

The souls who linger in this spot, some say, are here in eternal Limbo because they never learned the Silence of the Holy Ghost.

It's not surprising, since they're new converts to Christianity.

Paranormal Activity: **Souls**

Address: **Corner of Calle 61 and 66th Street, Centro**

Classification: **Benign**

The Possessed
✠ Convent ✠

he Casa de las Artesanias, the vast handicrafts market operated under the auspices of Yucatán State, on Calle 63 in the historic Centro, is located in one of the oldest buildings in Mérida: the city's first convent.

The first group of nuns moved into the vast complex, named the Convento de la Concepción, in June 1596. Some 267 years later, in 1863, it was seized in an anticlerical expropriation. This was consistent with the liberal reforms of Benito Juárez, who was intent on reining in the power of the Catholic Church in Mexican civil society.

In the century and a half since the former convent has been in the hands of civic authorities, it has lived many lives. In its most recent reincarnation it houses the crafts market, a community center, and a continuing education facility. Classes from yoga to guitar, painting to dance are offered here and are open to the general public.

This is not to say, however, that the former convent is at peace with itself.

There are sins, and there are ghosts. There are crimes against life, and there is death. This is a building that keeps state officials up at night, a place of distraught ghosts and cries in the night. It is a building possessed by murders committed by the killer nuns who ran this place. Within its walls women confronted life-changing choices, decisions that often that scarred them for life.

It is a place that cannot let go of the souls of the innocents slaughtered and of women who made decisions that resulted, on occasion, in their own deaths.

When to amend for the offenses against God? Against society? Against our own best judgment?

It is necessary to recall that there was a time when euphemisms smoothed over the unpleasant realities of life. One of life's unpleasant realities is what happens when desire meets flesh. In centuries past, society imposed severe restrictions on the circumstances under which male sperm and female eggs could join in the complex, marvelous process of creating more members of our species.

There was a time when young women who violated social expectations of the conditions under which coital relations were permissible—and found themselves pregnant—faced few choices.

In Mérida, young women from well-to-do families who became pregnant out of wedlock would suddenly find themselves "ill." They were promptly taken to the Convento de la Concepción to be cared for by the nuns. If ever there was an ironic name for a convent, here it was!

The nuns would assess the situation at hand, and in many cases they advised on steps open to these unfortunate mothers-to-be. Few were in a position to keep their children. Fewer still were mature enough to conclude that they would have to give their children away after giving birth. Most were persuaded—after untold hours of prayer and repentance—that an induced miscarriage was the most prudent, convenient, and socially acceptable course of action.

The Convento de la Concepción thus became a place where abortions were conducted by nuns, a place where the blood of innocents soiled the hands of the brides of Jesus. It was, in essence, a house of horrors: aborted pregnancies; young women who died from botched abortions; and nuns engaged in what, according to their beliefs, were acts of premeditated murder.

Dead young women. Forced abortions. Killer nuns. When to amend for the sins against life?

For Yucatán State government officials today this legacy remains a challenge. The union that represents security guards is at constant odds with state government officials. Most union workers assigned to work at the former Convento request transfers when they are assigned as night watchmen at this Catholic house of horrors.

They report hearing the wails of young women. They insist that they hear the cries of infants. They swear there are unexplained screams.

Are they hearing the wails of young mothers whose babies were taken from them? Are these the spirits of infants killed while still inside their mother's wombs? Are they the screams of women in agony undergoing abortions?

33

No one can say with certainty.

What can be documented is the constant series of reports from those who work inside the building late at night. What is not in dispute is the number of transfers requested by the night watchmen who refuse to remain at this post after a short time on the job.

There are records of two exorcisms taking place at the old convent in the mid-1950s in attempts to release the souls of those who are believed to inhabit the wretched place. Both efforts apparently failed, since there continue to be reports of the building being haunted.

Is this a permanent condition, a Purgatory in Mérida's historic Centro? Or does this speak of the number of infants slain by nuns across the centuries who have yet to find rest?

The more time passes, the less the answer is clear.

Except at night.

That's when the cries of the innocent are heard.

Paranormal Activity: **Spirits**

Address: **Calle 63 between Calle 64 and 66th Street, Centro**

Classification: **Tortured**

The Ghosts of Santiago

The Souls of the Slain ✠ Infants ✠

n most days, if the sky is bright, vultures sun themselves atop the *espadaña* of the Church of Santiago the Apostle.

Mérida has many churches. This is the one favored by vultures. They perch and spread their wings as if to embrace that which cannot be seen. Many pedestrians have wondered what makes this church so appealing to these creatures that live by scavenging the dead.

Decades of speculation offer clues to the reason carrion find themselves attracted to this place, generation after generation. It may have to do with an unspeakable crime believed to have been committed in this place during the turmoil of the War of the Castes in the 1850s and 1860s.

If the tale is true, it tells of a crime that defies belief, a sin that transcends grace. Indeed, it is a legend that challenges faith in humanity and prompts fear of demonic possession.

The story begins with the great turmoil that gripped the people of Yaxcabá during the War of the Castes. During decades of unrest and uprisings, the ebbs and flows of violence and rebellion, Spanish families were forced to flee smaller communities, seeking the safety of Mérida. In one instance, one of the Spanish families living in the municipality of Yaxcabá decided to secure the safety of their children before they themselves abandoned the lives they had built for themselves. Their intention was to send their daughters to Mérida and, after putting their affairs in order, to join them there. The family had plans to continue to Sisal and then sail to Veracruz where they had relations.

This was the background against which the father escorted his daughters—twins—to the parish adjoining the Church of Santiago the Apostle. The teenage girls were entrusted to the care of a priest the family had known for years.

The sisters had only recently been feted at their quinceñera, a coming-of-age celebration commemorated when a girl turns fifteen that is analogous to the sweet sixteen parties or bat mitzvah ceremonies popular in the United States. The father stated that he intended to return with the rest of the family in a month's time, or no later than six weeks.

He kissed his daughters on their foreheads, thanked the parish priest, and left.

The father would never see his daughters again.

In a surge of violence that swept through Yaxcabá, the parents, along with other relatives, were slain. News of these killings did not reach Mérida for several weeks.

Meanwhile, in Mérida, the beauty and charms of the twin sisters were undeniable. The parish priest, a mere mortal, was unable to resist temptation. The Bible teaches in Matthew 26:41: "Watch and pray, that ye enter not into temptation: the spirit indeed is willing, but the flesh is weak."

The priest's flesh proved weak.

He had sexual relations with both sisters. Of greater consequence, both young ladies, who had not been told they were now orphans, became pregnant. They were sent

to the Convent of the Conception (Convento de la Concepción) on Calle 63 to be looked after by the nuns.

Trusting that their parents were to return, the nuns had no guidance or authority to intervene in the natural order of life. In other words, the sisters' pregnancies were not terminated.

The sisters, remarkably, both gave birth to twins. The spectacular coincidences—twin sisters each giving birth to twins a few days apart—was seen as divine intervention and was the source of much fanfare at the convent. Many believed it was evidence that God blessed the presence of the Spaniards in Yucatán.

Here it was: Spanish blood multiplying, as the Bible commanded.

News of these events agitated the parish priest, who grew fearful of scandal. He concocted a story, telling the sisters that their parents were overcome with joy and that their father had summoned them home to Yaxcabá. He told the nuns that they were to take care of the infants until their mothers returned with the rest of their family. The sisters were to depart at once, in the company of two Maya attendants.

If anyone questioned why the sisters, now young mothers, would have to return to Yaxcabá only to come back to Mérida with their families, there is no record. God's ways are, if not mysterious, then certainly illogical.

It was no mystery what would be the outcome of such a journey: certain death for the sisters and their attendants.

At the same time, there were questions. The archdiocese grew suspicious of the various reports reaching their office. Amid the confusion and disorder caused by social unrest, where scores of churches had come under attack throughout the peninsula, the news of twins giving birth to two sets of twins was exceptional. That there was no father of record for either set of twins was noted as an ominous omission. That these sisters were in the care of a parish priest and not their parents was a minor detail that required further clarification.

It is at this point that there is speculation that the parish priest, having been possessed by the demon Asmodeus, who rules over lust, went mad. Some claim the priest was evil incarnate, evidence that the Maya were right to burn down churches. Others believed that Satan came and took possession of this fallen man.

Who can say with certainty? God works in mysterious ways.

The priest commanded the nuns to bring him the four infants from the Convent of the Conception. He arranged to have them looked after in his private quarters in the rectory. He delayed responding to queries from the Archdiocese.

Mérida, during this time, was overwhelmed by a wave of refugees fleeing rural communities. Authorities, civil and ecclesiastical, were distraught at the uprisings spreading throughout the land. In this confusion, it is said that the parish priest planned his murderous deeds.

In what is believed to be nothing less than proof of demonic possession, he is said to have strangled each of his children, three girls and one boy. He was reportedly seen on the roof of the rectory. Witness accounts described him as climbing a ladder with a sack containing his murdered children. One account tells of him tossing their dead bodies onto the roof of the Church of Santiago the Apostle.

The parish priest then vanishes from history.

Some claim he freely went into hostile territory, toward Yaxcabá, where he, too, was slain in the uprising. One report has him fleeing along Calle 59-A, the principal road to the Port of Sisal at that time. Others claim he was seized by the demon Asmodeus and taken directly to Hell.

In the days that followed, vultures descended on the Church of Santiago the Apostle. The carrion devoured the human remains of the murdered infants.

There have been reliable reports that the Virgin of Guadalupe appears at this site.

It is said that these innocents' anguished souls remain over the Church of Santiago the Apostle and that the vultures are a reminder of their feast on the flesh of innocents.

It is said that as long as vultures rest on the *espadaña* of this church and other vultures circle in the sky, the souls of these four infants remain in Limbo.

Paranormal Activity: **Souls**

Address: **Church of Santiago the Apostle, Calle 59 and 70th Street, Centro**

Classification: **Benign**

✠ La Llorona of Mérida ✠

The legend of the Crying Woman, or La Llorona, is a familiar one. It is familiar because life follows a predictable narrative, an arc of human sorrow and self-delusion that speaks to us across the ages.

On Calle 59, at the Belle Epoque manse numbered 570, between Calle 72 and 74th Street, stands an abandoned building. An identical mansion is adjacent to it, housing a gallery and café.

It is, however, in the abandoned building with its dilapidated facade that this haunting takes place. The story tells of a mother heard crying, lamenting the death of the children she murdered. This is the legend of a ghost who searches for the children she drowned in a cenote, a narrative of love lost, of madness and remorse.

The story begins with chocolate, a chocolate fortune no less. These houses were built at the beginning of the twentieth century by a man who made a fortune opening the first chocolate factory in Mérida. He had two daughters, and to prevent one from becoming jealous of the other, he built two identical houses, one for each of them.

One daughter married well and lived a conventional life, which is to say a life of dignified conformity. Hers was a life that required surrendering desire. The world is full of people who resign themselves to live lives of quiet desperation. Isn't that what Henry David Thoreau said? He knew that most choose the path of least resistance, and like water, most elect not to resist fate but to flow like a river all the days of their lives.

"All this time, the river flowed, endlessly to the sea," Sting sings. The days of this sister's life flowed endlessly to the Sea of Oblivion.

In Yucatán, however, the rivers flow underground, in a vast network of subterranean streams and cenotes. It could be said that the conventional life led this sister to the underground rivers of emptiness as time passed, and she herself passed from this world.

The second sister is the one whose life is of interest. According to the legend that has come down the decades, she became a tormented soul lost in despair, a woman who defied social conventions by living her life on her own terms. In her defiance, a romance concluded in tragedy.

It began with the natural desire that arises from our loins by virtue of our physical beings. As this story took place in Mérida, located in the heart of the Mayab—land of the Maya—it naturally involved the arrival of those who came from Tenoch, contemporary slang for Mexico City, the Aztec capital back then and also now.

The Maya believe nothing good comes of contact with those who live among the Aztec.

It so happened that Carmela Molina, daughter of then governor Olegario Molina, invited this sister to a dinner party she was hosting for members of a delegation sent to Mérida by President Porfirio Díaz. At this dinner, the sister, an impressionable and provincial but very spirited young lady, was taken with a dashing member of the assembled guests. The capital of the country was an exciting place, he told her, and Mexico's railroad was linking the entire country to that vast capital, which had become the heart of the nation.

It was thrilling to consider such a life, he told her. There was nothing as exciting as the modernity of urban life: the Modern Age was an Age of Wonder. Or some such nonsense.

It was the impressionable woman's desire to see the world, to be among urbane and cosmopolitan elites of the nation, which led to passion. From that passion, a child was born.

It is worth noting that, at that time, the journeys of delegations from the capital took months. (In the United States, when the Senate sent a fact-finding mission from Washington, DC, to San Francisco, California, to gather information about a proposed exclusion act to bar Chinese from entering the country, it took that delegation seven months to make the round trip.) Some members of the delegation from Mexico City to Mérida had embarked on a yearlong mission.

It was in this context that scandal swirled. Carmela Molina was mortified. She believed that had she not introduced these young people to each other, their illicit relationship would not have taken place. The sister had been a virgin, and the visitor was engaged to be married. The visitor disappeared for a while as he continued to carry out the duties of his delegation. He promised to return to Mérida.

Months later, he was back, and he stayed at the home of Carmela Molina. The sister, who was now a mother, wished nothing more than to marry this man and return with him to Mexico City. There she would escape the malicious gossip that had branded her a woman of no virtue, the proof of which was the child at her breast.

This could not be. He was engaged to another, and he would not take the mother of his child with him—not that this stopped either of them from expressing their passion for each other once again. Another pregnancy resulted. Four months before she gave birth, this suitor returned to Tenoch, leaving the Mayab.

Twins were born, and a telegram was sent to notify the resident of the Aztec capital of the birth of these two additional children. The Mexican sophisticate sent a telegram back stating that he had married. He also said that a number of gold coins were waiting at the Bank of Mexico's offices in Mérida. The coins were intended to defray the expenses associated with the children. He concluded the message by stating he wanted no further communication from anyone in Mérida.

The young mother's family was on the verge of despair. Her father grew distraught. His daughter's virtue had been compromised, and now she was mother to three children.

Her mother was in seclusion, occupied in prayer and tending to the needs of her daughter's three illegitimate children.

The young mother, on the other hand, received the news of her lover's marriage to another woman with stoicism. "He cannot buy my happiness. He cannot pay for my sorrows," the sister confided to Carmela Molina.

Then, three weeks later, she took her children to a cenote near a hacienda on the road to Sisal. She drowned them, one by one, holding them down in the pristine waters of the refreshing pool. Water filled their lungs, and each innocent perished. Their mother claims to have prayed for their souls, and for her own. She left their bodies in the waters of the cenote. She returned to Mérida.

A month after her crime, unable to come to terms with her grief, she took her own life.

It is said that Saint Peter refused to receive her and demanded that she find her drowned children and return with their souls.

The cenotes are linked to the underground rivers. When the spectral mother returned to the place of drowning, the bodies of her children had been lost in the rivers that flow beneath the ground. She now wanders this house, calling for her children and crying.

Witnesses report hearing the sounds of a crying woman coming from this residence late at night. The cries are said to be especially mournful after tropical storms. The rainwaters flood the cenotes and the underground rivers swell, taking the bodies of her children farther downstream. Visitors to the gallery and café in the adjacent twin building report the inconsolable cries of a woman in distress late into the night.

The lamentation of the Crying Woman, La Llorona, continues into the early hours. It is the lamentation of remorse for a crime that cannot be undone. There are not enough tears in the world.

This does not stop La Llorona from breaking down in tears, night after night.

Paranormal Activity: **Ghost**

Address: **Calle 59 #570, between Calle 72 and 74th Street, Centro**

Classification: **Benign**

The Ghost of the Poisoned Lover

✠ ✠

His name was Antonio, an ancient name of Etruscan origin whose meaning has been lost to history. It is closely associated with Marcus Antonius who, for a time in the first century B.C.E., ruled the Roman Empire along with Augustus. It is also associated with the thirteenth-century saint Anthony of Padua, the patron saint of Portugal.

The man's last name was Salazar, a compound name, combining hall (sala) and old (zahar), and meaning the dweller of an established house or palace.

The Salazar name is fast associated with Santiago, and to this day there are businesses that either bear the name or are owned by the family.

Whether there is any relevance to the origins and meaning of his name, what can be said with confidence is that much can be discerned from the woman in this story: Rebecca.

Here is a story of love and of lovers, a story of expectations made then dashed—a story of a man who was seduced by his love for a woman.

Antonio Salazar, a married man with two sons, grew enchanted by the laughter of Rebecca. She made him feel young. She made him laugh. She made him happy with the songs she sang for him. She had studied in Havana and brought with her the joy of the Caribbean.

It was the 1950s and Santiago was filled with the music of Latin jazz. Rebecca, fluent in Portuguese, favored bossa nova and samba, both genres popular in Brazil. Her rendition of "The Girl from Ipanema" proved legendary. Her take on Antonio Carlos Jobim and João Gilberto captivated Antonio Salazar.

In time, the lovers would meet with great frequency at the house located on Calle 74 and the corner of Calle 57.

Lovers believe, foolishly, that they possess time. Love makes them believe they can stop time. They convince themselves their love is strong enough to be eternal.

Rebecca grew more brazen, by which the world means possessive. She had Antonio, but she wanted Antonio for her betrothed.

"If you love me, you will leave your wife," she said as the 1950s were about to pass into the realm of history. "And you will marry me."

Antonio Salazar laughed off the suggestion in a gentle manner.

In the world and the time in which they lived, such things were impossible. A man had a wife, who was proper and respectable. A man had children, who would carry his name and his genes into the future. A man had a lover to share his inner thoughts and to whom he could reveal his soul.

That was the order of things. Rebecca rebelled against the order of things. She demanded marriage. He could not give her that. Instead, he offered a trip to Havana, boarding a vessel for New York, and then a flight to Paris.

Rebecca was reluctant to accept the way of the world.

A short time afterward, her daughter was taken ill. The girl, child of a previous lover, had leukemia. Rebecca was devastated. Antonio stood by her side.

He would arrive at the hospital with food for her, knowing she refused to leave her daughter's bedside during her treatment and that she was famished. Her vigil was, of course, futile. Leukemia was a fatal condition, and before long the girl passed away.

When she died, Antonio was there to hold Rebecca's hand and to comfort her. It was into his chest that she buried her face in grief, his arms that held her and caressed her. Antonio remained by her side as they lowered her daughter into the ground. He did all these things for her, but he could not marry her. That's what he told her when she asked him again.

She looked at him before he left her to return home to his wife and children. She wondered what it was like to have the comfort of a family.

"I will not steal your glory," she said when she saw him the following week. "I will not bother you with intimate questions of family. I will not demand confessions."

"Thank you. And I will die with the word Rebecca on my lips," he promised her.

That would be enough, she said. "My daughter died with Mother on her lips."

She lied. She did not understand.

Jealousy is a spiteful demon. One psychic who walked through the house claims that jealousy possessed Rebecca.

She planned vengeance. If she could not have him completely, then no one would. It would be in this very house, the one that, years later, the owners would abandon. The house would fall into disrepair and be occupied by people who sold junkyard scraps. They would sell live monkeys and exotic turtles from a corner room fronting the street. Before any of that took place, however, this would be the residence where she would kill him.

With meticulous care, she assembled the poison she would need. With a deliberate manner she combined her alchemy in a favorite meal. With a smile on her face and tears forming in her eyes, she poured more poison in his drink.

He felt ill. She helped him from the dining room to the bedroom. "Lie down, Antonio," she said. "Rest will do you good." She cradled him in her arms as he succumbed to the venom running through his body.

"What? What have you . . . done . . . Rebecca?" he asked.

"Let me sing you a lullaby," she said. "I have pleaded to Saint Elizabeth of Portugal, with no success. She will not help me. I am still enraged, and I realize I will never be your wife."

Antonio gazed at her, confused.

"What?" he asked. "I was there for you when you were at your weakest, when you were distraught. What have you done, Rebecca?"

He lost consciousness.

"And I am now here for you, my love," she replied.

She laughed. She laughed as she lifted his body. She laughed as she rolled his corpse over, from their bed to the floor.

"I am gifted," she said. "I am gifted with love and with patience and with faith. I am gifted with the vengeance of my sex."

She smiled at him. "I have now conquered jealousy. Your life is the price I paid."

With love and with patience and with faith, she did him in. No charges were ever filed.

His ghost now lingers, wandering this residence. It is heard late at night whispering one word. It is not the name of his wife.

It is the name of his mistress: Rebecca.

Paranormal Activity: Ghost

Address: Calle 57 and 74th Street, Centro

Classification: Benign

The Ecstasy of the Moaning Whore

✠   ✠

This is one of those hauntings that make spectators question the nature of life, the afterlife, and what happens in the time in between.

A nondescript colonial home on Calle 72, number 469, between Calle 55 and 57 Street, is the site of a notorious story that dates back to the expansion of Barrio de Santiago in the mid-nineteenth century.

This was one of the first barrios, or neighborhoods, established after the founding of Mérida. It has a rich history and is where many immigrant groups arriving in Yucatán first made their homes. Cuban, German, Italian, Korean, and Portuguese waves of immigrants, each has left their legacy on the character of the neighborhood.

And as is common around the world, where one finds transients—strangers arriving in a foreign land with dreams and aspirations—one will find sex workers.

They say that this house was once, a century and a half ago, the home of a well-known madam who had a lucrative business as a one-woman welcoming committee for the new arrivals to town—provided they had the financial wherewithal to pay for her prizes.

Known as doña Caridad, she was said to have a regal voice and an enthralling bosom. She was renowned for her flamboyant style of dress, one that emphasized the Pre-Raphaelite ideal of the female figure. Her ample cleavage was often exposed, presumably to showcase jeweled necklaces admirers had bestowed upon her as presents. In the polite and conservative society that existed in Mérida,

however, she was ostracized, but it made no difference. In the Santiago neighborhood she was quite a vision, and many found her irresistible.

Decades passed, and as Samuel Butler noted in his novel *The Way of All Flesh,* there is something to be said for rebels against social hypocrisy. Indeed, it's hard to think of many other women who, living in Victorian times, would flaunt their sexuality and openly declare that sex was nothing if it wasn't to be enjoyed. Fewer still would openly rejoice that orgasms were evidence of the primoridal nature of unencumbered carnal pleasure.

That did not sit well in a time when sex was seen as necessary for procreation and little more. In short, Doña Caridad's lifestyle, almost reminiscent of Mae West's had Mae West been a Victorian-era prostitute, was exceptional.

This leads us to back to the haunting.

In one celebrated incident, a client's wife, suspicious of her husband's habitual journeys to Barrio de Santiago, followed him surreptitiously. That is how she learned of his infidelity—and where doña Caridad lived and plied her trade.

"Es aquí donde vive esa Gran Puta," she is said to have remarked. "This is where that Great Whore lives."

Distraught and betrayed, the wife confided in her mother, her sisters, and her parish priest. She wanted to exact vengeance on doña Caridad, but she was convinced to control her urges and be forgiving and benevolent. She resisted the natural urge to retaliate, although anger and thoughts of revenge continued to race through her mind.

It was then that, against the advice of her parish priest, she availed herself of a Maya midwife who promised to prepare a potion and a spell that would make things right.

After some weeks, the Maya midwife delivered a potion to the betrayed wife. "If you relieve your soul of thoughts of vengeance, and if you open your heart, then this will work," she instructed. "Take this to the house where the Great Whore lives and offer these words as you throw this powder on the front door. When the Great Whore returns home, it will be done as you have wished deep inside your heart."

The jealous woman did as she was instructed. She went to the house on Calle 72. She spread the powder on the door and on the front sidewalk. Then she uttered this incantation: "May God grant you the pleasure you have denied me!"

With that, the betrayed wife fled before anyone saw her on that street.

What could she have meant? What pleasure had doña Caridad denied this betrayed wife? The love of a devoted husband? The adoration of children living in domestic tranquility? The social respectability of a happy marriage?

Surely she wished none of these good and proper things upon doña Caridad.

It would be years later, after both women passed from this life, that the power of the spell became clear.

Witnesses report hearing the moaning of a woman in the throes of sexual ecstasy emanating from this house, usually around the middle of the month—the *quincenas*—and at the end of the month, the days when workers are paid and presumably can secure the services of prostitutes.

Here is the epiphany: Doña Caridad, by being in the business of selling sex, had deprived many proper Yucatecan women of satisfying sex lives. She had denied them the one thing they longed for most in this world: orgasms.

And, some claim, it is now the fate of the ghost of doña Caridad to exist in an afterlife where she enjoys one orgasm after another orgasm, moaning in ectsasy for all of eternity.

Paranormal Activity: **Spirit**

Address: **72 #469, between Calle 55 and 57th Street, Centro**

Classification: **Benevolent**

The Ghosts of the ✠ Slaughtered Women ✠

Where there is injustice, it is said among the Maya, there is a community in anguish.

This is a familiar sentiment, one that resonates with the fundamental human sense of what is right and wrong. In Deuteronomy 1:16 we are instructed: "And I charged your judges at that time, saying, Hear the causes between your brethren, and judge righteously between every man and his brother, and the stranger that is with him."

In more contemporary language there is the maxim: No justice, no peace.

This is a tale of a house that is haunted by two ghosts of two women who were slaughtered and whose killers have never been found.

There are no reports of noises coming from the residence, no reports of these ghosts trying to reach out to the living. Nor are there reports of malevolence. There is only their silent presence in the residence in which they were murdered.

The place is Casa Ricalde Zurita, located on the corner of Calle 68 and Calle 57, a little more than one block from the Church of Santiago the Apostle. The crime took place in August 1999 when four men entered the house and killed the women. It was reported at the time that the murders were in retribution for a considerable financial debt incurred by the victims.

Scores are settled among the nefarious in such fashion since time immemorial.

In this case, however, the house was abandoned. Some said the family of the women feared retaliation. Others claimed that the peculiar circumstances of the house—three sides face streets—created an exhibitionist residence, almost like living in a glass house. A few ventured that the women had no close relations.

What is not in dispute, however, is that in the years since the crime, ghostly silhouettes have been seen wandering the residence at night.

Neighbors have, on occasion, suspected teenagers of breaking into the house and hanging out. On arriving, the police report finding no one.

Yet sightings of the distinct shadows of two women wandering the interior of the home persist. Some witnesses report seeing the silhouettes and shadows run from the downstairs dining room to the upstairs. Others speak of shadows of the female ghosts running in circles, as if fleeing pursuers.

Skeptics have dismissed these reports as the imagination of bored or nosy neighbors with nothing better to do than call the police once in a while. Many of the naysayers note

that because there are no noises associated with the ghosts, the sightings cannot be real.

Authorities on the paranormal dispute the belief that ghosts always make sounds. Much has been made of the fact that police, who patrol downtown as part of their community watch, have seen shadows moving in the abandoned house and have pulled over to investigate, expecting to find vagrants or teenagers inside the house. But when they inspect the place, there is no one.

For now, the place is said to be haunted by the ghosts of the two women who were murdered here more than a decade ago.

What can be said with certainty, experts in the paranormal claim, is that the silhouettes of two women are seen to wander the house in silence, ghosts unable to break free from this world.

It is a silent haunting by lives severed from this world before their time, condemned to wander in silhouette, casting shadows on the walls of perdition.

Paranormal Activity: **Ghosts**

Address: **Calle 57 and 68th Street, Centro**

Classification: **Malevolent**

The Dancing Spirits
✠ of the 1920s ✠

Not far from the Church of Santiago the Apostle stands this Art Deco house, bewitched by gaiety and song.

Located on Calle 57, between Calle 66 and 68 Street, the house numbered 547 is a two-story property that boasts an elegant Art Deco facade. What is curious about the spirits that are believed to occupy this house is their close association with American visitors from a bygone era.

In the mid-1920s, on his way to Havana, Zez Confrey visited Mérida. He was one of the most popular American composers of Novelty Piano, a genre of music associated with ragtime. This music was all the rage in the United States before the Great Depression.

Later in life, Zez Confrey often said he had been enchanted by his visit to Mérida and Yucatán. He was in town shortly after two of his songs, "Dizzy Fingers" and "Greenwich Witch," became international sensations and inspired a generation of composers.

There is no record of where he stayed after spending four nights at the Hotel Itzá, located behind the Peón Contreras Theater. (That hotel is today a school.) Some speculate he stayed with Yucatecan friends in Santiago who were aficionados of his music. It is known that several noted Yucatecan musicians and composers lived in the Santiago neighborhood during this time.

What can be said with certainty, however, is that there are continuing reports of music emanating from this house late at night. Not just any music: Passersby report hearing "Dizzy Fingers" being played, and the distinct sound of dancing. They also hear the laughter of men and women and the clinking of glass as toasts are made.

Witnesses report hearing the frenzied Novelty Piano music played softly, as if coming from the back of the house, suggestive of a garden party on a terrace.

On occasion, others report hearing "Waltz Mirage," which was composed in 1927. This is problematic, because Zez Confrey did not return to Mérida after that song was released. It suggests that some other spirit is playing his music. Not everyone is convinced that it is another spirit playing the music, however.

Could it be that the ghost of Zez Confrey has returned to Mérida since passing from this life? (He lived in Lakewood, New Jersey, and died in November 1971 after a long battle with Parkinson's.) Several authorities are convinced it is Zez Confrey, particularly because, along with the music, one hears toasts being made in English.

Certain words and phrases heard by witnesses are consistent with American slang from the 1920s. Witnesses report the voice of a man saying, "Mérida is the bee's knees," meaning wonderful. The voice of an American woman is heard asking for more "giggle water," 1920s slang for alcohol. Another female voice is heard to say that the evening is the "cat's meow," which was used to describe something superb or excellent.

It's important to consider that, late in life, Zez Confrey grew nostalgic for his time in Havana and Mérida. He longed to return to warmer climates. With the onset of Parkinson's, it became difficult for him to live in Lakewood during the harsh winters as he found himself far less mobile than he would have liked.

Another piece of evidence to consider is this tantalizing clue: The dance parties and musical numbers heard late into the night have been reported only since the mid-1970s, after Zez Confrey died. Prior to that time, no paranormal activity was associated with this residence.

Is it possible that Zez Confrey's ghost has returned to Mérida? Has he returned with his contemporaries who delighted in their visit to this city? Are they carrying on in merriment and song in the city's historic center?

Once, Zez Confrey was enchanted by Mérida. Is it possible that today it is Mérida that is enchanted by Zez Confrey?

One final piece of the puzzle to consider: The residents of the house do not hear anything, or if they detect a faint noise, they believe it must be coming either from La 68, an outdoor movie house, or from the rooftop terrace of Casa Mexilio, both establishments about a block away from this haunted residence. Neither of those places, however, have dance parties—or play Amerian Novelty Piano music from the 1920s.

Make of it what you will, but don't be surprised if, walking down Calle 57 near 68 Street, just past midnight on a Friday or Saturday night, you hear the distinctive music of the 1920s being played for the enjoyment of spirits engaged in a dancing and drinking party, oblivious to the fact that they are no longer part of this world, but living it up in the one beyond.

And if you do hear the festivities, enjoy the music: It's swell!

Paranormal Activity: Spirits

Address: Calle 57 #547, between Calle 66 and 68th Street, Centro

Classification: Benevolent

The Ghosts of the
✠ Black Dogs ✠

I t is one of those stories that has its origins on both sides of the Atlantic, one of those legends that, over hundreds of years, remains constant.

In Yucatán, there is a legendary beast, the Huay-Chivo, a creature feared by Maya and Spaniard alike. The term itself reflects this history of fear: *Huay* (or *Waay*) is Maya for sorcerer or malevolent spirit. *Chivo* is Spanish for goat. The compound word, sorcerer-goat, describes a doglike creature with burning eyes.

In areas of Campeche, the term is Huay-Pec, since *pec* is Maya for dog. In other regions of Mexico, the Huay-Chivo is known and feared as a *Nahua* or *Perro Negro*. Both these terms also mean Black Dogs, ghosts of malevolent hounds from Hell.

A nocturnal apparition, the Huay-Chivo is a harbinger of death, described as taking the guise of a black hound with glowing red eyes. Mexican legends tell us these Perros Negros are believed to be shape-shifters and Satan's familiars.

Europe, too, has legends of Black Dogs. Said to be the ghostly manifestation of Satan's servant-hounds, these creatures appear during electrical storms, traveling in packs and, with their heightened sense of smell and glowing red eyes, seeking out victims. Commentators have noted that the Black Dogs resemble Cerberus and Garmr, hounds that guard the Gates of Hell in European mythology. In English traditions, the Black Dogs are said appear in places where executions have taken place or where children have been killed and devoured by animals. They are omens of impending doom.

The house on Calle 55, numbered 531, between Calle 64 and 66th Street, now transformed into a lovely residence with a graceful Art Deco design and cheerfully painted, is the site of one of the most enduring stories of the apparition of Huay-Chivo, or black dog, ghosts in Mérida.

Black Dogs are said to roam the gardens of this house. Visitors at Medio Mundo, a guesthouse next door, have reported seeing what they believed at first to be shadows of large dogs running in silence. They report being startled by these creatures' glowing red eyes. Other witnesses report the sounds of low growls and piercing howling coming from the property.

These Huay-Chivos—ghosts from the Underworld—are said to appear with frequency near the entrance to this house. And indeed, there is a story of tragedy associated with this house, and it is offered as the reason why the ghosts of the Black Dogs linger here.

It seems a family from Campeche rented this house for one year in the 1940s. They had a child, a young girl not yet ten years old. Her father was in Mérida to continue his medical studies, and her mother divided her time between her home and teaching Renaissance literature and Italian to college-age young women as a private tutor. The family had two gun dogs, English pointers, a popular breed in Yucatán at the time.

It was one of those weeks in Mérida when the temperature soars and there is no relief from the heat. The family filled the swimming pool. Over the course of that week they enjoyed cooling off in the pool in the early morning and late afternoon. The father was adamant that the dogs not jump in the pool. He insisted that they could be cooled down with the garden hose. From their own account it was fun to hose the dogs down. Like most dogs, their English pointers enjoyed being sprayed with water.

In the midst of this happy domestic scene, something no one can explain occurred.

On a hot summer day after a series of electrical storms swept through Mérida, the parents were called away, each on business. The child was left by herself for a brief period; another adult was expected to arrive within a half hour or so. The young Maya woman who helped the familty with domestic chores did arrive at the house on time. She entered the house. There was no one. She reported seeing both dogs outside in the pool. She was startled. She swore she placed the laundry down on the bed in the master bedroom and immediately went outside to get the dogs out of the pool.

As she crossed the yard, she claims that the animals she saw were not the family's English pointers. They were large black dogs, and when they turned toward her, their eyes were red, and they glowed like burning coal.

It was then that she made the discovery. The dogs were holding the family's daughter underwater.

The young woman screamed and ran out onto the street. Crying uncontrollably, she summoned help from neighbors. She warned that Huay-Chivos had possessed the property. She said that the young girl was in the swimming pool.

Neighbors ran into the house. Two women helped comfort and calm the young woman. Another neighbor ran to summon the father.

It was too late.

The child was dead, even though two grown men were said to have jumped in the pool without even taking off their shoes. The men reported that both English pointers were in the pool when they arrived. They did not report seeing the feared Huay-Chivos.

The parents were distraught. Their child had been killed. Dogs had dragged the young girl into the pool and held her underwater. She had been clawed, and there were teeth marks on her arms and neck. She had been held down deliberately and drowned.

The father ordered the pool drained. He chained the dogs to each other and had the ladder removed. He abandoned the dogs to their fate: exposed to the elements, deprived of food. He watched as they slowly starved, reduced to eating their own excrement and lapping up their own urine. He gazed upon them as they fought each other. When the dogs perished, he ordered the pool filled with cement, entombing the canine corpses.

It is then the Perros Negros, the Black Dogs, began to haunt this place.

There is speculation that, summoned from Hell, the ghosts of the Black Dogs were ordered to help the doomed dogs. They appeared at this property and, through sorcery, attempted to make it rain. The hope was that by summoning torrential downpours, they could have flooded Mérida enough for the pool to fill up and allow the dogs abandoned in the empty pool to flee prior to the dogs having perished.

The couple returned to Campeche. The owners of the house understood why the pool was filled with cement. They claimed they would have done the same thing. Where the pool once existed, a basketball court stood instead.

This history was forgotten, and the current owners remodeled the yard and the grounds.

The Huay-Chivos still appear here, however. There are reports that Ghost Dogs roam near this house just before electrical storms sweep through the city. Guests of Medio Mundo swear they have seen these massive creatures, their glowing red eyes searching, and report hearing terrifying howls in the middle of the night.

Did the English pointers murder the child? Or were the ghosts of Black Dogs responsible? Why are there continuing sightings of the Huay-Chivos in the vicinity of this house?

There is no question that apparitions of Black Dogs with glowing red eyes continue to be reported. At night. During electrical storms. On hot summer nights when the moon is full.

Should you hear howls, they might come from the English pointers in their agony—or could they emanate from apparitions of the Black Dogs?

Or they could be the premonition of the death of someone of unknown time and place, perhaps your own.

Paranormal Activity: **Ghosts**

Address: **Calle 55 #531, between Calle 64 and 66th Street, Centro**

Classification: **Malevolent**

The Ghosts of Santa Ana

The Ghoulish Spirit of ✠ Santa Ana ✠

I t is one of the most gruesome sights one can imagine, a spirit in distress that has been reduced by fate to a ghoulish creature, the presence of a spirit that is seen wandering in circles in Santa Ana.

At times, people who are waiting for the bus that stops on Calle 60 in front of the church of Santa Ana have reported seeing him. He stands near them, as if also waiting for the bus. They report that he is a monstrosity to behold. On other occasions he is seen wandering the plaza, moving slowly without saying a word. He is said to frighten small dogs that are being taken on a stroll by their masters.

The ghost is of a white man. His face is emaciated, and he is wearing clothes that suggest the mid to late eighteenth century. That would place him as a resident of Santa Ana when it was rebuilt in the 1760s and 1770s. Recall that Santa Ana dates back to the sixteenth century. A hundred years after it was first established, the church and adjacent buildings were destroyed during an uprising by the oppressed residents who lived in the area.

At that time, Santa Ana was comprised primarily of farmland, and it was worked by Maya, blacks, mulattoes (people of European and black parentage), and *chinas cambujas* (people of black and Maya parentage). These constituencies lived in conditions that were slavery in everything but name. During a series of uprisings, the neighborhood was leveled. The present church was rebuilt in 1776.

The plantations that were adjacent to the church, which today are the residential neighborhoods around Santa Ana and most of Paseo de Montejo, operated as fiefdoms. The plantation owners made up their own laws, issued their own coins that constituted currency for the community that worked for them, and acted as sovereigns. The ghost that wanders Santa Ana is believed to be that of a Spaniard who was a plantation master who held men and women in bondage.

Two psychics claim to have made contact with the ghost and communicated with him. He identifies himself as the master of twenty-seven slaves, which would make him among the wealthier residents of Santa Ana in mid-eighteenth century Yucatán.

The ghost describes a furious uprising against his authority. The blacks and mulattoes he held in servitude overran the hacienda that stood two blocks northwest of the corner of Calle 60 and Calle 45. He describes being seized by a group of his slaves. He describes the betrayal of two of his most trusted and beloved slaves who joined the unlawful mob and rebelled against his authority.

"I loved them more than I loved my horse or my dogs," the ghost communicates. "They were like my own children."

His slaves did not hold him in such high esteem. They dragged him out of the hacienda and threw him in the horse's trough, where he struggled not to drown. Then they took him to the cellar of the hacienda, where machinery, equestrian equipment, and unused furniture were stored. They shackled him to metal bars, placed a bucket of water within reach, and bolted the door shut when they left.

There is nothing to indicate this man was crueler than other slaveholders, nothing to suggest that he was singled out for greater retribution. What is known is that the *hacendados* felt privileged, and they ran their affairs as they saw fit. In fact, during this time the area was formally incorporated into Mérida to prevent the Spanish landowners from conducting their affairs outside the jurisdiction of civic authority and oversight.

The ghost claims his slaves had never renounced their confidence in the faith of their African fathers, and they saw this uprising as deliverance. As they shackled their master, they told him that his own countrymen would rescue him—or he could avail himself to the deities of his faith.

"They tied me as if I were mad," the ghost has communicated to clairvoyants who have reached him. "They left me without food. That is why I had no choice."

The ghost explains that no Spaniard came looking for him, and after a couple of days he began to pray to San Pedro Claver Corberó, known as Saint Peter Claver to English speakers, the patron saint of slaves and African Americans. Born in 1580 in Catalonia in Spain, Saint Peter Claver is remembered for stating, upon entering the religious life, "I must dedicate myself to the service of God until death, on the understanding that I am like a slave." He subsequently arrived in New Spain and worked as an advocate of slaves, principally in the city of Cartagena in New Granada, which today is Colombia.

The ghost explains that he offered to become a "slave" of Saint Peter Claver if he were delivered from the desperate circumstances in which he was abandoned by his runaway property.

His prayers were not answered.

"I had no choice," the ghost explains, with regret. I had to eat."

He offers no other explanation. He does not elaborate on the hunger he felt, the desperation of the pangs, the thoughts of madness that ran through his mind.

I suppose I did not mention it. Yes, I did report that this ghost, emaciated and distressed, was a ghoul. But I did not mention why.

This ghost engages in autosarcophagy.

I'll spare the gentle reader the bother of looking it up: Autosarcophagy is self-cannibalism.

It appears that his former slaves shackled this man in life and abandoned him. In desperation, he began to eat his own forearm.

This ghost wanders Santa Ana periodically, biting portions of flesh from his forearm as if it were a drumstick. He has eaten it to the bone, and his wrist and hand are a dark greenish-gray, suggesting the onset of gangrene.

Should you find yourself in Santa Ana and think you see what appears to be a zombie, don't be afraid. It's a ghost from the eighteenth century who has been wandering Santa Ana for centuries, every once in a while tearing a bite of flesh from his forearm for sustenance.

A master abandoned by his thankless slaves has to eat, doesn't he?

Bon appétit.

Paranormal Activity: **Spirit**

Address: **Church of Santa Ana, Calle 60, between Calle 45 and 47th Street, Centro**

Classification: **Malevolent**

The Murmuring Demon of Santa Ana

A constant noise in the background of one's consciousness, a soft murmuring and whimpering, the sound of an eternal demon that has endured across the ages is heard coming from this possessed house. It is also the horror that appears in the dreams of those who live in the wretched dwelling. They report dreaming of an old, emaciated woman. Her weakened voice cries softly, almost as if she were being abused or feared being struck.

A former resident swears that the house is inhabited by the ghost of an old woman who starved herself to death. This man, who lived in the house located on Calle 62, numbered 369-E, between Calle 43 and 45th Street, claims that she would appear to him in his dreams, telling, in fragments, a story of a mother forgotten and neglected, abandoned by her daughter.

The ghost claims that her daughter had turned her back on her moral duty to take care of her, and she was left alone. The ghost tells of her decision to end the suffering by starving herself.

"One day I decided I would simply no longer eat," the ghost revealed to the former resident in a dream. "And I slowly starved myself to free myself from the loneliness and neglect in which I suffered."

Several authorities concur that this kind of situation, in which a person ends the pain of neglect by starving to death, results in the suicide's ghost haunting a new resident's dreams.

And in their waking hours the living hear a constant murmuring, a background hum of whispering and whimpering, and perhaps sense the presence of vultures overhead. Some say it must be a ghost, but these people are few. Most observers believe it is Murmur, a demon who is a great duke of Hell.

If they are right, then a demonic angel arrived at this house on the back of a Great Vulture. Murmur takes two common forms: himself, wearing his ducal crown, dressed like a soldier and riding on the back of a vulture; or he shifts shape to appear simply as a vulture.

He is said to have descended here, waiting for the ungrateful daughter who abandoned her mother to an old age of neglect and willful starvation. That is the most common explanation offered. Residents of this place have reported a constant voice, the sound of the demon Murmur calling out "Medusa" or "Medina" or "Mentecata."

Many spiritualists believe this is no less than the house of a fallen angel, the demon Murmur, who has been

invoked by the presence of a woman who comes to residents in their dreams to lament that she was forced to starve herself to end the pain of having been abandoned by a wretched daughter.

Do you dare enter this place?

Paranormal Activity: Ghost

Address: Calle 62 #369-E, between Calle 43 and 45th Street, Centro

Classification: Malevolent

The Ghost of the Dead ✠ Daughter ✠

I t started with a kiss, an innocent kiss between a young girl and a classmate. Only a kiss.

This kiss awakened desire, the natural longing of two youngsters in the throes of becoming aware of the changes in their bodies as they become adults. She rested her hand on his shirt after he made a silly joke. It led to a kiss.

It was the 1940s.

"It's killing me," he said. "The way you make my heart feel."

"That's the price you pay for being a silly boy." She laughed.

It was only a kiss.

She ran off, or she'd miss the bus. She smiled at him as she looked back and was gone.

A brief digression is in order. The human female displays few signs of fecundity, a fact that has not been satisfactorily explained by evolutionary biologists. This concealed ovulation is especially confusing during puberty; it takes time for women to learn to recognize their level of fertility.

For this schoolgirl, the kiss led to daydreams. What was it about this dreamy boy that made him so dreamy? What made her eyes so eager when she saw him? Why did her chest rise? Why did she find herself laughing uncontrollably in the early morning when she held a garden hose in her hands and watered the plants on the terrace and in the gardens of her home?

She lived in the house on Calle 62, number 369, between Calle 43 and 45th Street, now closed for years, uninhabited by mortals. It would be the site of great despair and turmoil.

Her family was not from Yucatán. They were from the Valley of Mexico, interlopers in the Mayab, the land of the Maya. What the girl did not know, nor could she have known, was that she brought with her the blessing of Mayahuel, the Aztec goddess of plants and flora.

When the girl was born, the goddess laughed as she lifted her out of her cradle and chose her alone. She kissed the girl on her forehead, and with that kiss, Mayaheul gave her the gift of flora and fertility.

The schoolgirl's mother marveled at her gift with plants. "All you have to do is smile in a plant's direction," she would say, "and the next day, it will bloom. What a green thumb!"

It had only been a kiss from the goddess Mayahuel.

Here in the Mayab, with love and with grace, this young woman was finding her way, making friends and excelling at school.

"Life has certainly smiled on you," her mother would tell her. "But that doesn't mean you have permission to smile back at the boys who smile at you."

She laughed it off, putting the hose away, picking up her books, and rushing off to school. The schoolmates met during recess and flirted.

This was the Mayab, and the exuberant presence of an Aztec deity was unwelcome in the Yucatán.

That night she could not sleep. What was it about this boy's kiss? She stood by her bedroom window and looked on the garden illuminated by the moonlight. She went to bed. Moonlight filled her room, and the candles placed next to the framed image of the Virgin of Guadalupe were illuminated by the heavenly orb.

Her mind was filled with thoughts, profane thoughts. She wondered: What would it feel like? Would she dare?

The girl rose from her bed, walked over to the dresser, and picked up a candle. She returned to her bed. She pressed the candle against her sex, and she closed her eyes as she felt pleasure. She moaned slightly, growing distracted.

Her mother, unable to sleep that night, was in the kitchen.

Some say Ah-Pukuh, the Maya god of death, had awakened the mother. Others say it was Ixtab, the goddess of suicides, who made her way into that home. All believe that the Maya deities would not allow an Aztec interloper to thrive in the Mayab.

The mother heard soft moans coming her daughter's bedroom. She stood at the door and listened.

Then, without knocking, she opened the door. She caught her daughter pleasuring herself with one of the candles used to honor the Virgin of Guadalupe.

"What are you doing?" she screamed, turning on the light. "Are you mad?"

A second and final digression is in order. Adolescent masturbation has been a major concern throughout the Western world for centuries. It was only during the Industrial Age that people believed there could be remedies perfected based on science. In Europe, António Egas Moniz, a Portuguese doctor, invented the lobotomy, one purpose of which was to cure aberrant sexual behavior. In the United States, John Harvey Kellogg, a doctor who ran a holistic sanitarium, invented a cold cereal to suppress sexual desire. Kellogg believed that chronic masturabation was a medical condition in which the "victim literally dies by his own hand." There is, however, no evidence that threats of performing lobotomies or a bowl of Kellogg's cereal do much to suppress teenage sexual desire.

The mother ran over, grabbed the candle from her daughter's hand, and then slapped her across the face.

"You sinful girl!" she screamed. "You're filthy!"

Spiritualists say the room filled with light, as if in flames. They say Mayahuel appeared. The Maya believe that Mayahuel had to defend her envoy in this foreign land.

Some say Mayahuel cursed the mother: "It is your hand that will bring forth death! It is your hand that will make the flora wither!"

The mother's name was Lucila, which in Latin means bringer of life. The Aztec goddess now reversed her place in the world: Lucila would turn flora lifeless.

It is said the mother's face aged a decade in that instant. Others claim she first placed her hand on her chest, falling back at the sight of Mayahuel. Was her heart the first thing that died in that moment? Her hands were cold. Her skin grew ashen. Was she any longer human?

What is not in dispute is that the mother, enraged at her daughter's blasphemy, ordered her lobotomized. In the world in which they lived—ithe 1940s—chronic masturbation in females was, on occasion, cured with bilateral prefrontal lobotomies. In the United States, one of the more famous cases was that of Rose Williams, sister of the playwright Tennessee Williams.

In the weeks that followed, Ah-Pukuh, Maya god of death, plotted vengeance. The power of Aztec deities had to be expelled from the Mayab. The Maya deities conspired against the power of the Aztec goddess. And in Maya mythology, suicide by hanging is an honorable death, a welcome sacrifice to the gods.

Ixtab, the Maya goddess of suicide, remains active in Mérida. To this day, Yucatán has the highest suicide rate in Mexico.

One night, Ixtab appeared before the girl. Ixtab kissed her on the forehead. Ixtab helped her hang herself. Ixtab accompanied her to paradise.

The power of the Aztec goddess Mayahuel was thus banished from the Mayab. The mother, Lucila, however, remained cursed, bringing death to the flora she touched.

It is said this house is possessed by the ghost of a dead daughter. Her laughter resonates from the world beyond, a mocking echo of the fecund life she could have brought but that the world was denied.

It is a haunting, taunting laughter that ends with the sound of a kiss.

Can you hear it?

It is only a laugh. It is only a kiss.

Paranormal Activity: **Ghost**

Address: **Calle 62 #369, between Calle 43 and 45th Street, Centro**

Classification: **Benign**

The Haunting in the ✠ Secret Dungeon ✠

Every street has one, doesn't it?

A sexual degenerate. If your neighborhood doesn't have some sexual degeneracy going on, consider yourself unfortunate.

Then again, it's one thing to be sexually adventurous, and another to be a sick person. Where is the line drawn?

The ambivalence of where the line is drawn is as ancient as the Old Testament. In Nehemiah 13:2 we learn: "Because they met not the children of Israel with bread and with water, but hired Balaam against them, that he should curse them: howbeit our God turned the curse into a blessing."

This is a story of damnation, not so much about ghosts or souls as about curses. It is the story of a Maya incantation bewitching a place. Some say it involves a demon of despair, but others believe it to be a curse. What is certain is that the essence of the house located on Calle 66, numbered 399, between Calle 45 and 47 Street, is haunting.

Hidden behind walls, there are more walls in this house. As originally built, one set of walls opened onto a room used for sexual adventure. In contemporary language, this room would be called a dungeon. In the language of the nineteenth century it was referred as the Master's Dab, a place where one could "dab" it up, meaning engage in carnal acts, with complete abandon.

The descendants of the owners, who have subsequently sold the property, were circumspect about the nature of the haunting. They declined to offer information other than what is in the public domain. The shame of sexual perversion transcends generations.

The nature of this shame, of this curse, of this reluctance to keep a property, speaks of the evolution of sexual mores and the nature of a haunting derived from carnal excess.

The story begins with adventure and reflects the social upheaval in Mérida during the War of the Castes, when many people of Spanish ancestry abandoned the peninsula for safety. One such resident, an engineer by profession, fled to the United States, a nation also in turmoil as attitudes hardened around the peculiar institution of slavery and American society became polarized.

Civil war loomed in the United States, but there were tremendous opportunities for those who fled the eastern seaboard and headed west. The railroads were booming, and there were fortunes to be made by the ambitious and educated.

This is how the Mérida resident who fled civil war in Yucatán found himself fleeing civil war in the United States and landed in the Rockies as a railroad engineer. This world of the frontier, of building civilization in the wilderness, of strangers thrust together—some for economic opportunities, others for adventure, most fleeing civil war—resulted in a more fluid sense of morality and permission.

It was here, then, amid Victorian conventions of corsets and garter belts for women, frock coats, silk vests, and derbies for men, that sexual license was possible. In a journal entry dated May 11, 1891, reflecting on his time in the United States a quarter century before, one finds this confession: "I needed to think bigger. I needed to be brasher. I needed to let go of convention."

Then the story unfolds, one of finding a mistress and incorporating fantasy into an active sex life. It is a tale of a man's journey into eroticism, where the accoutrements of equestrian life became instruments for carnal excess. In the stable, with lashes, whips, harnesses, saddles, sisal ropes, leather binding, stacked hay, and privacy, fantasies could be fulfilled. Simple tools—the inclined plane, the pulley, and the wheel and axle—led to a vigorous sexual life.

The fantasies lived out with his mistress included erotic humiliation. Bondage, discipline, spanking, extended periods of orgasm denial, submission to his dominant. These were the areas of role play and perversion that were discovered in the American West. These were the sexual mores introduced into this house when he returned to Mérida. In this residence, the well-appointed stable for the horse-drawn carriage disguised a well-appointed dungeon for illicit sexuality.

A man's fawning over his horse disguised his passion for perversion.

In his own journal he noted that, in the years of sexual excess, one crime was committed here. It was an incident in which a mechanical prop came asunder; a young woman suffered the consequences of sexual misadventure. She was struck by a pulley, hemorrhaged profusely, and died.

Months later, upon learning the nature of his daughter's relationship with the man in whose house she lost her life, the young woman's father vowed vengeance. They say he became distraught beyond consolation, and so the father of the dead young woman summoned a Maya shaman to place a curse on this residence.

The hedonist was not entirely aware of the nature of the curse, but he noted that his neighbors were alarmed when the incantations were performed on the sidewalk outside his home over a period of several weeks.

His journal entries subsequent to that unfortunate incident reveal, however, that the sexual fantasies of the owner were frustrated. He suffered from one physical condition or another that made it impossible for him to perform or to explore his sexuality with his prior abandon. Once renowned for the erotic humiliation he endured at the hands of his dominant, as gossips whispered behind his back, he now withered.

The journal reflects a growing dementia, with the writer asking himself existential questions reflecting disorientation: How did I get here? How do I work this? Are the days slipping by? Why does water flow? Who carried the water to the ocean? Where is my magnificent mistress? Am I right? Am I wrong? Who carried the beautiful water to the ocean? Where is my beautiful dungeon?

A few years after the curse was placed, the house became infamous; people said there was a haunting and that this residence was the House of Frustrated Orgasms, and the people who lived there were unable to enjoy happy sexual lives.

Two generations later, the house was sold and remodeled, but the curse is said to endure. It haunts the building in order to protect innocents from danger. It is said that this is a house where those who engage in sexual adventure will find sexual misadventure.

Is there evidence that the curse continues?

There is one place with a definitive answer: the Police Department. It turns out that there are police reports detailing criminal complaints of sexual fantasies gone awry at this address. There are police reports detailing assaults, beatings, and physical altercations as well as police reports documenting sex crimes—and unspeakable erotic humiliation.

This place is the only bewitched residence in Mérida associated with sexual misadventure and a sadomasochistic curse.

Is it really the House of the Frustrated Orgasm?

Who dares to spend the night in the House of the Frustrated Orgasms to find out one way or another?

Paranormal Activity: **Ghost**

Address: **Calle 66 #399, between Calle 45 and 47th Street, Centro**

Classification: **Malevolent**

The Tortured Soul of
✠ a Distant Suicide ✠

Not everything that happens in Vegas stays in Vegas.

That much is clear if one believes the sighting of the tortured soul of a young man crying out in the night.

The story tells how a boy-king became a distraught young man. It's a story of a lost child abandoned by his parents, first by divorce and then by indifference.

Not much is known about this tortured soul, but there are clues.

He is not Mexican but American. And he haunts Mérida because this is where his search for his father has led him. Those who have heard his voice report that he asks one question in Spanish: *"¿Sabes de mi padre Santiago, que me abandonó en busca de revolución?"* This sentence—"Do you know of my father, James, who abandoned me in search of revolution?"—is heard in a soft, pleading voice.

No one knows what to make of it. What kind of man would abandon his own son? What foreigner would come to Mexico as a modern-day Che Guevara to foment rebellion?

There are other pieces to this puzzle that offer clues, however. The ghost appears at the entrance, or in the interior terrace, of the Casa del Panadero, in the historic Centro. He is seen nowhere else in town. He wears a black T-shirt, with a skull painted in gray. It has a single sentence written on it: My Suicide Is My Revenge.

Some witnesses report the ghost also wears sunglasses and a baseball cap. There is a simple word embossed on the cap: Vegas.

There are those who report that his voice cracks at times, almost as if this lost boy, searching for his father, is about to cry. Witnesses report that when he asks if anyone knows the whereabouts of his errant father, the ghost's voice quivers.

The Maya believe that suicides will travel great distances in search of peace. And that once they arrive at the place of their sorrow—and become visible to the living—they will remain there for all eternity until their pleas are answered.

"Do you know of my father, James, who abandoned me in search of revolution?" the tortured soul of a distant suicide pleads to the living, abandoned once more.

The Maya who venture past the Casa del Panadero often make the sign of the cross: To be abanoned in life by a parent is a sin, and to be abandoned in death compounds the horror of this tortured suicide.

No one knows the whereabouts of James, the man who abandoned his suicidal son in distant deserts.

No one, not even the tortured soul of this lost suicide.

Paranormal Activity: Soul

Address: Calle 49 #511-B, between Calle 62 and 64th Street, Centro

Classification: Malevolent

The Anguish of the Spirit of the Titanic ✠ Mourner ✠

*I*magine for a moment living in a home where, inexplicably, you are awakened in the middle of the night by the sound of plates being smashed against the floor. Now imagine going to the kitchen to find shards of dishes strewn about.

Skeptics would say that a dish simply fell off the kitchen counter. But what if the pieces of the shattered plates were not like the dishes you owned? The design and color are like none of your own dishware?

This is the predicament that the family that lived at the once-proper house located on Calle 64, numbered 451 (between Calle 53 and 55th Street) experienced for decades. Today the house is little more than a stone facade and ruins, locked and waiting to be sold.

There is a story behind the broken dishes.

The story involves a young woman's anguish and grief over the fate of loved ones aboard the RMS *Titanic*, which sank one hundred years ago the year this story is being published: April 15, 2012.

A century ago, the RMS *Titanic* struck an iceberg in the North Atlantic Ocean and sank, sending 1,517 people, including some of the wealthiest people in the world, to their death in the icy waters. Two of those passengers were bound for Mexico City, and five were en route to Havana,

Cuba. From there, two were scheduled to continue on to Mérida a few weeks later.

The first-class passengers bound for Mexico City were Manuel Uruchurtu and Arthur Gee, who first met as passengers aboad the doomed ship. Both men drowned. Of the five bound for Cuba, one, a first-class passenger, was named Servando Ovies Rodríguez, and he, too, drowned. The remaining four passengers heading for Havana traveled in second-class accommodations, and all survived: Julian Padrón Manet and Emilio Pallas Castello and two sisters, Asunción Durán Moré and Florentina Durán Moré.

These sisters were scheduled to continue to Mérida later in the spring of 1912, when the weather is driest in Cuba, which is during the month of May. They were scheduled to meet with their intimate, a certain Leticia, a cousin of the Duráns.

News of the sinking of the RMS *Titanic* reached Mérida by telegraph in a matter of hours. At that time, news traveled fastest when sent by telegram. The telegraph office was located downtown, where the Museum of the City is currently housed. It still operates today as a post and telegraph office.

In the confusion following the sinking—it would take more than a month for the manifest to be reconciled with the list of known survivors who were scattered along communities throughout the American northeast—it was presumed that both sisters, Asunción and Florentina, had perished. As it turned out, both sisters survived by finding passage aboard Lifeboat #12.

It was the presumption of their death, however, that led Leticia to madness. Unable to control her anguish, she crying and screaming ran to the kitchen and smashed the china against the paste-tile floors., they say it took three adults to calm her down and prevent her from hurting herself.

In the days that followed, in her inconsolable grief, Leticia confided to her mother the anguish she suffered for her relatives: Hers was a "special" friendship for the sisters. It was, in essence, a common euphemism for lesbian desire.

Despite the conservative nature of Mérida's society, it allows for much discretion. This is a city where one of the most successful businesswomen, doña Carmen Barbachano, owner of the Casa del Balam Hotel, is openly gay and several women politicians are frank about their orientation. A century ago, a young woman like Leticia would face social scorn not for her sexuality but for lack of discretion.

When her mother's suspicions were confirmed by her daughter's admission and unbearable grief, it proved difficult for the family to understand fully the nature of Leticia's behavior. She was said to be living in a room empty of furniture. She was said to have smashed all the windows. She was said to have cuts on her feet from walking on broken glass.

For days Leticia was in despair. She confided that the wreckage in the watery grave of the North Atlantic could not compare with the wreckage of her heart. And she was said to be so despondent that she smashed the family's living room mirror and, with a shard, slit her wrists and bled to death. Her body was found in her bedroom amid a pool of blood and broken glass.

A week after Leticia's death, another telegram reached Mérida: Asunción and Florentina were among the survivors and would soon be on their way home to Havana. The two sisters, upon learning of Leticia's suicide, were overcome with remorse.

Their three-way lesbian affair had been exposed, and the family had been shamed not by homosexuality but by the suggestion of incest and suicide. Both sisters remained in Havana, married well, and lived their lives.

Leticia's suicide would not be the only heartbreaking event originating in Mérida to touch their comfortable lives. They would be uprooted decades later in their old age by another Cuban who embarked to Havana from Mérida: Fidel Castro.

For Leticia, the news of the sisters' survival reached Mérida too late, of course.

Throughout the decades that have followed, there have been reports of dishes and glass being shattered against the paste-tile floors. And in the morning, on occasion, without any explanation, there are shards of broken glass in the kitchen of this abandoned property, abandoned long ago... and yet still occupied.

Paranormal Activity: Ghost

Address: Calle 64 #451, between Calle 53 and 55th Street, Centro

Classification: Benign

The Singing Spirits of the Aluxes

✠   ✠

here is something to be said for a joyful haunting.
On Calle 56, numbered 476, between Calle 49 and 51st Street, witnesses report hearing singing—joyous singing that resembles a chorus of enchanted spirits.

In Maya mythology, an alux—the plural in Maya is aluxob, in Spanish *aluxes*—is a mischievous creature. If they are treated with respect, they will bring you good luck.

93

When the Spanish first arrived in Yucatán and encountered the aluxes, they considered them to be a kind of *duende*: supernatural creatures analogous to goblins. And not unlike goblins, aluxes have the ability to engage in all kinds of activities, short of casting spells.

For most of the twentieth century, witnesses have reported seeing aluxes jumping up and down on the roof of this building. At times they dance with one another. Regardless of how many there are, or if they are dancing, they are always singing. Aluxes sing a cappella, and in a language that no human being understands. Consequently, while witnesses report seeing them dance and hearing their singing, no one quite knows what the content of their songs is.

Their singing, however, is a fortuitous omen. Several authorities are convinced that the previous owners of this residence were kind and respectful to the aluxes. This usually means recognizing their existence and their right to live among people. "It usually entails making them feel comfortable in a residential garden," one psychic explained. "Few people allow an alux to have free reign in their gardens, so they move pots and plants around to discourage them. But if you let them accommodate your garden to their liking, then they will reward you for respecting their wishes by bringing you good fortune."

The consistent reports of singing aluxes on the roof of this house is a joyful omen for the residents of this building.

Can you hear them after dusk? Have you heard the aluxes singing each to each?

Can you hear the faint a cappella songs they sing?

If you can, you are among the lucky.

Paranormal Activity: Spirits

Address: Calle 56 #476, between Calle 49 and 51st Street, Centro

Classification: Benevolent

The Ghost Horses of
✠ Paseo de Montejo ✠

For years, patrons who drop by the Impala Café late at night, usually on their way home after an evening out, have reported hearing the distinct whinnying of horses. Nearby residents also report the faint but distinct sound of galloping. And the soft whisperings of a man's voice.

Some believe that these sounds are the result of the late-night horse-drawn carriages that walk up and down Paseo de Montejo with tourist passengers. Others attribute the sounds to active imaginations. People swear they hear these horses long after the horse-drawn carriages have retired for the evening. What is peculiar is that people only report hearing these horses at the south end of Paseo de Montejo. The carriages normally venture all the way north to the Monument to the Flag.

The truth is that there is reason to believe that ghosts of long-dead horses linger at the beginning of Paseo de Montejo. Few know that, for several years halfway through the project, the construction of Paseo de Montejo was suspended for lack of funding. Without streets or a median, the boulevard was a wide venue. And here, for a brief period, horse races took place.

General Francisco Cantón, who later built the largest mansion on the boulevard—today it houses the Regional Museum of Anthropology and History—was governor in 1902, when he authorized horseracing to take place on Paseo de Montejo. .

The races were frequent, and betting was allowed. Well-to-do Meridians, like proper Edwardians around the world, made much of the sport, and in this spirit spectacular races unfolded. Some of the equestrians were noted horsemen from Barcelona, since Cataláns were enamored with Mérida, and many sailed from Barcelona to Havana and then continued to Progreso in order to reach Mérida.

In what otherwise were celebrations of equestrian showmanship and civic gaiety, a horrific incident occurred. During one of the concluding races of the season in 1902, several horses were spooked by fireworks, bolted, and jumped into the viewing stands. Three children were injured, and one young man was trampled and lay mortally wounded.

This accident caused great alarm among the spectators and brought a somber conclusion to the day's festivities. The priest from Santa Ana was summoned immediately so that he might administer last rites to the dying youth.

The resident priest being absent, another cleric, visiting from one of the parishes in the historic Centro area, arrived quickly. Upon realizing, however, that this event included the placing of wagers on the horses, he grew furious. "It is retribution for the sin of gambling," he was overheard to say. "This was not an accident but punishment for this sinful assembly."

The youth's mother begged the priest to relent and and have mercy on her son. He refused to administer the last rites to the dying man, whose last gasps were not enough to move the priest to show compassion. The priest further demanded that the horses that had bolted onto the viewing stands be put down.

The young man died moments before doctors reached the scene. All they could do was attend to the children who had been injured and calm the nerves of the distraught ladies who had witnessed this calamity.

It was then, as the young man's mother held her dead son's body in her arms, that she looked up at the priest and issued this curse: "It is you who are sinful, and it is you who will never leave this place, which will become your Purgatory for eternity."

With that, the priest abruptly turned and left, feeling no need to offer a retort to a delirious woman's ramblings.

And yet, a century later, there are reports of people hearing the whinnying of horses, the galloping of horses, and a man's voice whispering: "Through this holy unction and His own most tender mercy may the Lord pardon thee whatever sins or faults thou hast committed."

Is this evidence that, upon his own death decades later, that priest's soul never left this earth and wanders the southern area of Paseo de Montejo, as if in his Purgatory?

Many believe so. Indeed, the phrase one hears is, in fact, part of the last rites he denied the injured man, and evidence that a mother's curse reached the ears of God.

Paranormal Activity: **Ghosts**

Address: **Paseo de Montejo between Calle 47 and Avenida Colón**

Classification: **Benign**

The Ghost of the
✠ Slain Infant ✠

his is the nature of the world, the way life unfolds. It's no secret that great crimes arise when passion overtakes reason. What appears to be insurmountable at one moment will, with the passage of time, however, take on a far different perspective.

The scent of one's love lingers in our reptilian memories even if, decades later, you have all but forgotten a name. Isn't that so?

As Alan Jay Lerner and Frederick Loewe wrote in their famous song, "I Remember It Well." "We met at nine—We met at eight." The couple bickers. The man recalls being on time. The woman reminds him that he was late. He ignores her correction, singing that he remembers it well. They agree to disagree on their conflicting memories. Alas.

In recognition of our human frailty and the malleable nature of memory, the story of the infant ghost of the Casa del Minarete can be told.

This manse, built at the beginning of the twentieth century by Dr. Álvaro Medina and numbered 473 on Paseo de Montejo, harbors a dark family history. It centers not on the good doctor but on his brother, Miguel Medina, who is believed to have supervised the construction of this astonishing home.

"I'm not crazy," Miguel is believed to have confided to his brother Álvaro, years after the house was built and the world was reveling in the abandon of the Roaring Twenties. "I'm just a little unwell. I've been possessed by melancholy."

The source of his emotional anguish, whether it was insanity, being unwell, or simple melancholy, was no doubt the guilt he felt over an incident that haunted him for all the days of his life, a tawdry affair with a young servant girl named Rosario. Then there were the crimes he committed to hide evidence of this affair.

Sleeping with a servant girl? It should surprise no one, since this is a dilemma as old as the Bible. Exodus 22:16, King James Bible, states: "And if a man entice a [maiden]that is not betrothed, and lie with her, he shall surely endow her to be his wife."

But what if a man already has a wife? And what if a man lives in a society where there are prohibitions against having multiple wives?

It is rumored that it was in this house that Miguel Medina seduced a servant girl, who became pregnant. His brother, Álvaro, both the master of the house and a physician, took care of the pregnant servant, ensuring that her pregnancy was out of view and that the young woman was looked after.

When the child was born, however, attitudes hardened.

The young Maya servant, Rosario, was taken to a distant village and left in the care of relations. They described her as having been diagnosed with psychosis and needing to be sedated. There is no record of what became of her in the years that followed. She vanished from the written record.

There is also no official record of the birth of the son she bore. It is believed the infant remained in the house in Mérida, hidden from the world. He was never baptized and never given a name other than the one spoken by his mother in her prayers and in her loss.

What is known, however, is that the two brothers argued. Then the infant disappeared one night. It is said that Miguel Medina surreptitiously entered Álvaro's home while he was away and took the boy. It is said that he smothered the infant. It is believed that he disposed of the body in the cenote that existed in the front gardens.

Didn't you know? There was once a cenote in the gardens of this gracious home.

The Casa del Minarete was sold by Dr. Álvaros Medina's three adult children—Álvaro Jr., María Luisa, and Virginia—in 1971. Extensive renovations were undertaken, including filling in the cenote in its entirety. The gardens were covered with asphalt. Where flowers once graced the home, there is a parking lot. The cenote, sealed like a tomb, now has a guard house over its entrance.

The regional office of Axtel, the telephone service provider, now occupies the house. A security guard booth stands where steps once led to the underground well.

And what do you suppose passersby report hearing late at night when they walk past the gates that separate the street entrance to the parking lot and the front staircase?

That's right: The muffled cries of a child being suffocated.

There are witnesses who report the anguished cries of a man, as if hyperventilating, sobbing. Others report hearing a distinct lamentation: *"No tengo otra,"* "I have no choice."

But you and I both know that these voices are mistaken, for in life there are always choices.

Then again, tell that to the ghost of the infant boy who gasps for air from his grave, deep inside a cenote that has been filled in with asphalt along the elegant Paseo de Montejo.

Paranormal Activity: Souls

Address: Paseo de Montejo #473, between Calle 35 and 37th Street

Classification: Benign

The Apparition of the
✠ Mourning Mother ✠

For most of our existence as a species, mothers had to learn to mourn the death of their children at an early age. Our family trees are littered with relatives in centuries past whose children died in infancy. Almost certainly no one alive today can tell of a grandparent or great-grandparent who did not lose a child in infancy.

The wealthy were not spared these tragedies. Along Paseo de Montejo one finds the Casa Vales, number 483-A, between Calle 35 and Avenida Pérez Ponce. Although the house, now the regional offices of Santander Bank, was christened by Augustín Vales, he did not build the mansion.

The house was built for Fernando Rendón in 1905, and later sold, in 1914, to Señor Vales, who then gave the mansion to his son, Carlos Vales, on the occasion of his wedding to Rosa Cámara.

The privileged newlyweds promptly moved in and settled into a life of comfort. But wealth is not a guarantee against tragedy. The couple had three sons, only one of whom survived to become a grown man: Miguel Ángel. The first two sons, Carlos and Oswaldo, died in early childhood.

In those times, it was customary to have infants and young children buried on the grounds of a house, provided permission was secured from municipal authorities. Oftentimes this was granted, provided there was ample space to carry out such a request. It is said that doña Rosa was so distraught at having lost one of her sons at such a tender age that she could not bear to have his body buried at the Vales family mausoleum. Instead, the child was interred on the grounds, with a shrine and garden built as a memorial. They say she visited his grave every morning to pray and offer flowers.

Decades pass, and so do memories. Life goes on for the living, and in the natural order of things, both Carlos and Rosa passed from this life. Their surviving son grew into a man, and who could expect him to mourn the death of brothers he never knew?

When the property was sold to the bank, the house was restored to its original splendor. The gardens and the grounds, however, were another matter. A modern office building was constructed—and it was connected to the original mansion by a glass atrium. The gardens became a parking lot for employees and clients and also housed supporting structures for the modern bank's operations—a building for security guards, another for ATMs for public use, and so on.

In the course of these renovations and new construction, the small crypt was found. The family was notified. The remains were transferred to the family mausoleum.

This was all done in an efficient manner, consistent with contemporary bureaucratic norms. That is to say, no religious ceremony was conducted to provide a sense of continuity and decorum. It is perhaps this violation of respect for the dead that accounts for the strange occurrences reported by people who visit and work in this compound.

Bank employees are said to hear, late at night, a woman's voice asking, "Where is my child?" or "Where have they taken my child?"

Witnesses describe seeing a woman's figure in the windows of the second floor of the mansion near the end of October and the beginning of November. There are frequent reports of soft sobbing on November 1, the Day of the Innocents, when Mexicans commemorate the death of infants, who are believed to have died in a state of grace and thus are without sin, save original sin.

Perhaps because they are more sensitive to a mother's grief—or perhaps because the apparition seeks them out—more women than men report hearing this pleading voice and seeing her presence. Female bank employees who work late report that, upon walking through the parking lot, they feel the touch of a hand on their shoulders, but when they turn around there is no one.

Nothing except the voice of a woman asking for her child.

Is it possible that the apparition is the soul of doña Rosa looking for the grave of her lost baby boy? Is it a mother's grief across the decades that implores the living for an answer? Is she destined to continue walking among the uprooted gardens of her former home looking for the garden and shrine that she, in life, ordered built for her child?

No one knows.

What is certain is that in this most modern of office buildings, there is the lingering voice of a mourning mother whose grief endures, and who is sensed by the living.

It is, many believe, evidence of the enduring power of a mother's love.

Paranormal Activity: **Soul**

Address: **Paseo de Montejo #483-A, between Calle 35 and Avenida Pérez Ponce**

Classification: **Benign**

The Catrina in the
✠ Horse Carriage ✠

his is one of the most enduring apparitions in the imagination of contemporary Mérida.

There is no doubt that she is a source of wonder. At the sight of her, the old make the sign of the cross and the young delight in the possibilities of life.

We are talking of sightings of a *calesa*—a horse-drawn carriage—striding along Paseo de Montejo with no passengers. A Catrina holds the reins of the horse in her bony hands.

She is said to be dressed in brilliant colors and to be wearing a fanciful black hat. Her veil moves in the wind as the carriage sweeps through Paseo de Montejo.

The Calavera Catrina, or Elegant Skull, is an image created by José Guadalupe Posada in 1910 at the start of the Mexican Revolution.

Intended as political commentary mocking the bankrupt materialism of Mexico's elite during the Edwardian Age at the end of the dictatorship of Porfirio Díaz, the *Catrina* represents an upper-class woman turned into a skeleton. It was meant to embolden Mexico's disenfranchised masses to fight for social justice, and to be an arresting reminder to Mexico's wealthy that their aspirations were vacuous vanities.

Over the decades the image of the *Catrina* (female) and the *Catrin* (her male consort) have become associated with Day of the Dead (Halloween) on October 31, and the

Catholic religious holidays All Souls Day (November 1) and All Saints Day (November 2).

In Mérida, the *Catrina* at the helm of the empty *calesa* is seen as a ghostly manifestation of ridicule of the excess of the Paseo de Montejo. It is a mocking reminder that these grand homes have all but been abandoned by the families that built them. Only a small number of the mansions remain occupied, most prominently the twin houses located on the south part of Paseo de Montejo, the Casas Cámara.

These mansions, numbered 493-A and 495 on Paseo de Montejo, between Calle 43 and 45th Street, were built by Ernesto Cámara and his brother Camilo Cámara at the beginning of the twentieth century. The mansion numbered 493-A belongs to the Molina Chauvet family. The other, numbered 495, belongs to the Barbachano Rul family. In March 1968, Jacqueline Kennedy was a houseguest of the Barbachano Rul family and spent several nights there. The structures are in slight disrepair today.

With these notable exceptions, the vanities of Mérida's elite vanished in the course of the twentieth century.

When did the *Catrina* begin to appear on Paseo de Montejo?

The first sighting was reported on August 1982. That was when Mexico suffered its worst economic crisis since the Great Depression. The devaluation of the Mexican peso at that time impoverished multitudes. It accelerated the flight from the grand homes along Paseo de Montejo by families who suffered a drastic diminishment of wealth.

Witnesses report that the *Catrina* appears along Avenida Colón at some indeterminate location between Calle 60 and 62nd Street. She seems to appear out of thin air. Upon reaching Paseo de Montejo, the *Catrina* turns right, that is, south, onto Paseo de Montejo.

She is said to stride gaily, striking poses, as she moves down Paseo de Montejo. On reaching the *Remate* (Calle 47), she turns and heads back north, until reaching the intersection where the Vips Restaurant is located. She is

109

said to then turn right, onto Avenida Pérez Ponce, and then vanish once more. Into thin air?

Witnesses are uniform in their description that her presence is one of gloating, as if to make the point that while the mortals who raised these structures are gone, she endures.

Some reports indicate the *Catrina* will stand in the *calesa*, move her arms in a theatrical manner, and mock: *"Casas abandonadas! Abandonadas casas!"* In other words, she gloats, "Abandoned homes! Homes that are abandoned!"

There it is, but is this interpretation correct? Is she Mérida's Immaterial Ghost?

Make of it what you will. Should you, however, find yourself strolling along the Paseo de Montejo late in the evening and spot what appears to be a mad bride-to-be or a lost participant of some bachelorette party gone wild, don't be so sure.

It could very well be a *Catrina* mocking the foolish vanities of mere mortals.

That, gentle reader, includes your vanities.

Paranormal Activity: **Ghost**

Address: **Paseo de Montejo, between Calle 47 and Avenida Colón and Avenida Pérez Ponce**

Classification: **Benign**

The Ghost of the
✠ Demon-Bird ✠

At the north end of Paseo de Montejo one finds the astounding Monument to the Flag. Constructed between 1946 and 1957 by the Colombian sculptor Rómulo Rozo, it is remarkable in scope and a popular destination among visitors to Mérida.

It is also the place of a haunting. Directly to the northeast of this monument one finds the Villa Donata, a mansion constructed by Pedro de Regil. The house was inhabited by his descendants, the Peón de Landero family, until 1928, when it became first the Conciliar Seminary and then the offices of the archdiocese. In 1960 the house reverted back to residential use. In 2005 the current restaurant, El Portón, opened.

The one resident whose presence endures across time immemorial is Vucub-Caquix.

Vucub-Caquix is a Demon-Bird in Maya mythology. He is depicted as a large creature, half vulture and half condor. A malevolent being, he severed the arm of one of the Hero Twins with his sharp beak.

The ghost of this Demon-Bird is seen floating in silence as it circles the area between the monument and the Villa Donata.

The Maya believe these structures—the Monument to the Flag and Villa Donata—stand over a hidden entrance to the Underworld. They say that Vucub-Caquix guards the entrance from infidels and that the presence of nonbelievers has unleashed the Demon-Bird to watch, wait, and protect the Underworld from the profane.

In recent years the apparition of Vucub-Caquix has been mistaken for a UFO. With his arms spread wide and his propensity to glide in a circular motion above the stark monument and the trees fronting Villa Donata, he resembles a dark saucer in the heavens.

More terrifying than the sightings of the Demon-Bird, however, are the reports of animals disappearing in this vicinity. It is suspected that the voracious creature swoops down, extends his powerful talons, and grips dogs and other animals to devour them in the trees.

A horrific incident of a young mother taking her children on an early evening stroll was recorded in 1962. She claimed to have come under attack by a giant bird that swooped in and extended its talons. It reached for one of her young sons and disappeared with the boy.

No trace of the youngster was ever found.

For reasons unknown, the ghost of Vucub-Caquix patrols these skies, in silence.

If you are here late at night, look up. And stroll with caution.

Paranormal Activity: Ghost

Address: Paseo de Montejo at the Monument to the Flag

Classification: Malevolent

The Haunting of
✠ Itzimná ✠

he first copy of *Malleus Maleficarum*, which in Latin
means "Hammer of the Witches" and was written
by Heinrich Kramer in 1486, is thought to have
reached Mérida in 1598.

It is not clear why it was brought to Yucatán. There is
no recorded request for it by Juan de Izquierdo, bishop of
Yucatan at that time. There is speculation that Gonzalo de
Salazar, who would serve as bishop from June 1608 to
August 1636, might have wanted a copy of it.

How it arrived in Yucatán is not as important as the fact
that it did arrive in Yucatán.

The book explains that three fundamental elements are
necessary for witchcraft or sorcery to unfold. Foremost is
the presence of a witch or sorcerer intent on pursuing evil.
Second, Satan's assistance is necessary. Finally, God must
grant permission. (God granted humanity free will, and
that being the case, everything must be allowed; God grants
automatic permission for any sin to take place.)

It is against this knowledge that the author makes a
forceful argument that witchcraft does exist. And if it does
exist, it can be prosecuted as a crime. Then the author
classifies the varieties of withcraft that exist in the world,
and how the faithful can combat each one. The author
concludes with legal advice to assist judges and
ecclesiastical authorities on how to prosecute the witches
and sorcerers in their midst.

It is a wonder this book is not a perennial best-seller on Amazon.com, given the state of the world.

Centuries before Amazon.com existed, however, the parish of Itzimná was founded. At the time—1752—it was a town a short distance from Mérida. Today it is fully incorporated as part of Mérida, a few blocks from Paseo de Montejo.

Records tell us that a certain José Rodríguez Martínez was living near that parish in the 1760s. He is said to have become enamored with *Malleus Maleficarum*. He claimed it was all he wanted. It was all he needed. It was everything he wished for.

What did he mean by that? Some say he meant that this book was the blueprint for fighting the witchcraft and sorcery the Maya insisted on practicing. Others claim a more malevolent reading: This book would help him avail himself of witchcraft and sorcery in order to cast spells on the Maya shaman who resisted Christianity.

No one knows. What is known is that he became obsessed with this book. How was it possible for God and Lucifer to collude to permit evil in the world?

What was it about evil that intrigued him so much? Did destiny call him?

It was, after all, only a book. But what a book!

"There's always some other thing to uncover," he wrote in his journal. "There's always more knowledge to discover for the sake of our faith."

Incantations followed prayer. Prayer followed incantations.

It is said he chose to surrender control. Was it jealousy? And if so, jealousy of whom? God, who relinquished responsibility by letting evil flourish? Or Lucifer, who enjoyed God's tacit blessing?

In one horrific episode, José Rodríguez Martínez went to the Church of Itzimná on a Sunday. After Mass, he walked outside and turned around to confront parishioners.

"I will grant you all protection from evil!" he shouted. "I am invincible against evil! I have become everything you wish you could be!"

Onlookers made the sign of the cross and walked away, unsure of what to make of this spectacle.

It is then that José Rodríguez Martínez began to walk in circles, speaking in Latin. It is said that he then swirled as if in a trance, moving his hands over his head, then threw an unknown white powder into the air.

"I want your affliction!" he whispered.

"I want your adoration!" he asserted.

"I want your vengeance!" he projected.

"I want to surrender to you!" he shouted.

There is debate as to what happened next. Some say flames appeared out of nowhere, not unlike spontaneous human combustion.

Others state that the smell of sulfur filled the air.

There is general agreement, however, that they heard the voice of the fallen angel Lucifer. They say he uttered one sentence, and one sentence alone: "I now possess your soul."

Did José Rodríguez Martínez vanish in a pillar of smoke? Many people would have wished him to disappear forever.

On the other hand, did Lucifer make himself manifest in that moment?

No one knows.

What is undisputed, however, is that since that time, the a ghost of a man is seen wandering outside the church of Itzimná. He walks circles around the church, a tall man with his mouth hanging open and his tongue hanging out like a dog's. He drools saliva, which is green.

His green saliva is said to demarcate the inviolable space of the Church of Itzimná so as to protect this parish from the spells a Maya shaman cast centuries ago to drive the Europeans away.

His saliva smells of sulfur as it drools from his mouth. Its putrid green is the color associated with decay and death in medieval Europe.

It is said he is Lucifer's Human-Dog patrolling this place.

"I mean nothing to you," he is heard to growl in a low voice to passersby. "I don't know why."

Do you know?

Do you know why he means nothing?

Paranormal Activity: **Ghost**

Address: **Church of Itzimná, Calle 19 and 20th Street, Colonia Itzimná**

Classification: **Malevolent**

The Ghosts of Parque de las Americas

The Two Ghosts of ✠ Villa María ✠

illa María, across from the Double Tree hotel, is one of the most elegant homes on Avenida Colón. It doesn't take much to envision its splendor during its heyday. The residents of this house clearly enjoyed a life of privilege and refined comforts.

That was decades ago, though, and today, after decline and abandonment, this grand home sits forlorn. And it prompts us to ask the question: Why are there ghosts in residence?

There is nothing in the history of the house to suggest paranormal activity, and it is only the passage of time and the diminishment of wealth that explain the conditions of neglect that now characterize the structure.

Nevertheless, there are persistent stories that the house is haunted. Witnesses report seeing a female ghost, an elderly woman. She is said to be dressed in a white dress with ruffles around the collar and long sleeves. It could be an elegant nightgown or a fancy dress from a bygone era. The ghost is always silent. No one has reported hearing voices.

She is said to appear in the eastern doors (to the left as one faces the house from Avenida Colón). Witnesses report that her face is smooth as silk and her expression is, if not haughty, then at least cool and distant as air. Others report seeing curtains gently billowing and the flickering of candle flames. Impossible, since the house is closed up. The windows are secured shut and no one could possibly be lighting candles inside the residence.

It is almost as if she is waiting for someone to come home—as if she is looking for someone and she believes that a casual passerby might be the person for whom she waits. This ghost of an elderly woman dressed in white and standing vigilant by the window is the one most often seen and commented upon by pedestrians walking past the house.

That isn't to say that she is the only ghost to inhabit the house.

Witnesses report the presence of another, less benign spiritual presence. Also a female, she is dressed in a dark red and purple coat. She is said to appear on the second-floor balcony, her hands on the banister as she stares down at the sidewalk. She too is silent, although periodically she will open her mouth and stick out her tongue, which is green.

No one knows quite what to make of this apparition. Is she mute? Has her tongue been disembodied and become gangrenous? Is her intent to plead for help? Or to curse?

Witnesses report seeing her when the moon is bright, and an hour or so after midnight. She is said to walk in a circular motion, her hands on her head, as if in pain. Then, abruptly, she will walk to the edge of the balcony, place her hands on the banister, lean forward and stare out onto Avenida Colón, and stick out her tongue.

What is peculiar about both these apparitions is that one ghost appears from inside the house, looking out, and the other is always outside on the second-floor terrace. Some have speculated that the ghost on the balcony is lost, not realizing that the soul on the first floor is looking for her. At the same time, the ghost in white is unaware that the spirit for whom she waits might be upstairs, locked outside on the second-floor balcony. There is also the opinion that the two spirits inhabit different dimensions, each unaware of the presence of the other, which would make the house doubly possessed.

This is a reasonable conclusion, given that several generations have lived in this mansion and that the nearby area is known for paranormal activity. What is also known is that the current owners have a difficult time keeping caretakers. Many night watchmen report hearing strange noises and unexplained presences. Many refuse to spend the night on the property.

Here is another tantalizing fact: When renovations began across the street to convert the house where the Double Tree hotel now stands, several workmen quit, reporting seeing a ghost dressed in red and purple and hearing wailing. Some witnesses claimed to fear becoming possessed by her. The night workers feared that they would go insane and lose their minds.

A Maya shaman was brought in to purify the place and give the ghost permission to depart. Perhaps she did, but it is precisely around this time that the second ghost on the balcony began to appear across the street. Did the ghost simply cross the street? Many believe so.

Is it possible that the first ghost, dressed in white, looking from the first floor of Villa María, is staring across the street, horrified by the abomination that has been constructed? Is the ghost on the balcony the one that was chased away from across the street by the Maya shaman? Is that why she stares from the balcony and sticks out her tongue at the hotel that has been constructed where her former residence once stood?

There is this thrilling speculation: She hates what they have done to her former home and today stands on the balcony of Villa María to taunt her persecutors.

Who knows?

What is clear, however, is that Villa María is one of the few haunted places in Mérida that is possessed by two distinct ghosts, neither of which seems to be aware of the other's presence.

Paranormal Activity: **Ghosts**

Address: **Avenida Colón #508-J**

Classification: **One ghost is benign; the other ghost is malevolent.**

The Ghost of the
✠ Missing Narco ✠

This is an account of what is believed to be the most recent haunting in Mérida. It centers on the disappearance of a young man who was believed to be involved with the narcotraffickers—narcos for short—from the northern part of the country.

It has nothing to do with *Santa Muerte*, or Saint Death, the patron saint of the narcos. But it has everything to do with the ghost of a young man. He is so tormented that he cannot find peace and depart the world of the living.

It is hardly surprising that so little is known about him. Narcos, for the most part, do not lead lives that are open books. In this case, there are only a few known facts, the barest of bones with which to flesh out a man's life, and his afterlife as a ghost.

What is known is that his name was señor Manzano, and he was a native of Mexico City. It's also certain that he worked for a "businessman" from a troubled border state. It's been established that he was responsible for looking after his boss's interests in Mérida.

The last known fact is that one day, while he was having lunch with three other men, two SUVs pulled up outside the restaurant. Three men entered the restaurant. They walked directly to the table where señor Manzano was having lunch with his companions. He was asked to step outside. He didn't object or resist and did as he was told. The four men then got into the second SUV and it drove away.

No one ever saw señor Manzano again. He joined the ranks of Mexico's disappeared.

Witnesses, however, now claim to see his ghost in the predawn hours.

Neighbors report seeing an apparition resembling señor Manzano lingering near the house he rented on Calle 17, between Calle 18 and 20th Street, two blocks from Park of the Americas. Witnesses recognize him because the ghost wears ostrich-skin boots and belt and a white shirt tucked into black military-style combat trousers. He also sports a black cowboy hat. Other witnesses disagree. They report that the ghost wears a "narco polo," a stylish Ralph Lauren short-sleeved polo shirt, the open-neck jersey with the familiar oversize polo player on horseback swinging a raised mallet.

There is agreement that he wears expensive gold rings on his right hand and a bright gold chain.

The ghost's sartorial preferences aside, his torso is said to be riddled with bullets and there is a gunshot wound in his forehead. The ghost is silent, but he wanders the streets near his home, walking back and forth to the Park of the

Americas as if in a trance. In the park, he paces back and forth along the fountain located behind the Biblioteca José Martí.

Some believe that, in time, he will speak.

Others believe the bullet wounds have silenced him forever.

Only time will tell.

Paranormal Activity: Ghost

Address: Calle 17, between Calle 18th and 20th Street, and Biblioteca José Martí, Parque de las Americas, Colonia García Gineres

Classification: Benign

The Ghost of the
✠ Entombed Maid ✠

I t is something out of a horror movie, one of those tales reminiscent of the stories favored by Vincent Price.

You remember Vincent Price. He was the American actor who established himself as a force in horror movies in 1939 when he starred with Boris Karloff in *Tower of London*. Now that's a film you may want to include in your Netflix queue. At least check it out on YouTube.

If you want to meditate on a tale of true horror, the next time you find yourself in Mérida try wandering around Parque de la Americas. Take a stroll south. On the northwest corner of Calle 18 and 27th Street stands a grand house that has been completely remodeled. Only the front of the house reminds one of the charming home it once was. The expansions, consisting of vulgar nouveau-riche walls upon walls, have diminished its appeal.

Three quarters of a century ago, however, this house was *swell*, a gracious and perfectly respectable residence. And it was home to a troubled man who was possessed by melancholy.

This story concerns the burdens he carried within his soul. Readers need not concern themselves with the politics that led to his anguish, for that part of the story is boring. What is of consequence is the stoicism that characterized his life and the mental breakdown that led to the anguish he suffered.

His was a stoicism that led to silence.

"Speak to me," his wife would plead. "Your silence fills me with fear."

He would not speak.

"What worries you?" she would ask. "Let me know what hurts you. How can I help you heal?"

Some say that he lost a fortune during the Great Depression. Others claim he mourned the death of his son, who died in Palestine in 1938 in the Arab Revolt against the British Mandate. It was a peculiar set of circumstances that led his son from Yucatán all the way to the Holy Land to fight against the occupation of the Levant by the British. It was folly, and it ended in death, filling a father with grief.

"Look in my eyes," his wife pleaded.

"I do. I see that you, too, are hiding tears," he replied.

The couple grew apart. His troubles tore their marriage asunder. The wife would find excuses to leave Mérida. She would visit family here, she would visit friends there. She would go on excursions overseas. She would busy herself with charitable endeavors for the betterment of this or that.

All the while, he was left alone, except for Guadalupe, the maid who attended to domestic chores.

"I will build something," he said one day when his wife told him she would be leaving on a trip to Mexico City.

He began to build a thick stone wall with a hollow space within. Some say he wanted to defend himself from the troubles of the world. Others say he was going mad. His wife became distraught as she witnessed this compelling obsession. The maid watched in silence, making sure the linens were washed, provisions were purchased at the market, and the house was kept in order.

The disorder of his thoughts intensified, however. So did the mourning for his dead son. The father's melancholy was like a series of waves washing ashore, one upon the other. A new obsession took hold and led him to bring several goats onto the property.

"Speak to me," his wife pleaded one day after breakfast.

"Destiny is my duty," he replied.

She was unconvinced. She felt misled. He went outside to continue building his stone wall. She looked at him as he lifted a bucket filled with tools. She turned to Guadalupe and said, "I feel a storm of rage swelling. If you need to

127

find shelter from the storm, you have my permission. Flee if you must!"

He continued to work on his enigmatic wall. At night he would pray and wail for his dead son.

"I will be back in nine days," his wife told him as she prepared for a visit to relatives in Mexico City.

"Leviticus sixteen eight," he replied.

She left.

Leviticus 16:8 reads: "And Aaron shall cast lots upon the two goats: one lot for the Lord, and the other lot for the scapegoat."

It is followed by: "And Aaron shall bring the goat upon which the Lord's lot fell, and offer him *for* a sin offering. But the goat, on which the lot fell to be the scapegoat, shall be presented alive before the Lord, to make an atonement with him, *and* to let him go for a scapegoat into the wilderness."

In the Hebrew Bible, the demon Azazel is generally depicted as goatlike.

There are conflicting versions of what happened in the days that followed. Some believe the man went mad. Others say he was possessed by Azazel, whom he blamed for his son's death. He would murmur to strangers that his son had been slaughtered in Palestine like an innocent goat offered on the altar of futility.

What is not in dispute is that he would complete building his stone wall, rock upon rock. It is also known that he hung the picture of the Virgin of Guadalupe on one side of the wall and a cruxifix on the other. He also asked Guadalupe, the maid, to help him.

He asked her to step inside the hollowed-out space within the wall, needing her help to finish stacking the stones to complete his task. They worked through the morning, raising the last stones. At one point, some mediums speculate, Guadalupe asked how she was going to get out, since the opening was becoming smaller. It became more and more uncomfortable for her to work in that confined space.

"I won't trouble you with that worry," he is said to have replied.

She grew fearful. He grew manic, stacking the final stones and sealing them with cement. In a few moments and before she could react, he had entombed Guadalupe.

Then he walked away. He wandered into the wilderness of this world.

No one heard from him again. When his wife returned, she found the house abandoned.

When the wall was knocked down decades later, workers found Guadalupe's bones. That discovery was one reason the house was closed down, abandoned by its owners. It is not without irony that the current owners spent so much effort to build walls and walls and more walls as they built on to the existing home.

It should be noted that in the years that followed this grim discovery, Maya witnesses report hearing the anguished cries of a ghost. They believe it is Guadalupe. They claim her ghost lingers in the place where she was sacrificed by a father's unbearable grief. They hear her pleading to be let out. They hear her cries for help.

Can you hear her?

Are your sensibilities such that you hear the cries of a reluctant offering to the Lord thy God or to Azazel?

The Maya hear her ghost. The Maya hear the cries of the entombed maid. The Maya are aware of Christian sins perpetuated against them.

Can you hear the cries of the innocent?

Paranormal Activity: **Soul**

Address: **Calle 18 and 27th Street, Colonia García Gineres**

Classification: **Benign**

The Ascendance of the ✠ Demon Rats ✠

It is not a house, but a quinta, which means it occupies an entire city block. *Quinta* is translated "a fifth," and a city block is a fifth of an acre. In this residence in the middle of Calle 27 between Calle 16 and 18 Street in Colonia García Gineres, one finds a walled compound.

It is said that when this spot was nothing but a rural encampment it was visited by the incorrigible Spanish lord don Juan Jesús Díaz y Bahamonde, who spent time in Mérida in the 1820s and 1830s. At that time what is now Colonia García Gineres was uninhabited land held as communal property by various Maya villagers. It was, in short, primarily a wasteland comprised of tropical scrub forest. They say that don Juan Jesús Díaz y Bahamonde would camp out in the wilderness at this site to commune with nature.

Legend has it don Juan Jesús Díaz y Bahamonde delighted in the isolation of this place and in venturing forth in it. It is also said that he was taken by the occult and determined to diminish the power of Satan in the world. It is widely believed he would engage in a series of incantations reminiscent of sorcery. Others claim, based on writings he left behind, that don Juan Jesús Díaz y Bahamonde came to this spot to recite the beatitudes that Jesus Christ disclosed during the Sermon of the Mount.

Here, from Mathew 5:3–12, is a translation of what he would have recited:

130

Blessed are the poor in spirit: for theirs is the kingdom of heaven.

Blessed are they that mourn: for they shall be comforted.

Blessed are the meek: for they shall inherit the earth.

Blessed are they which do hunger and thirst after righteousness: for they shall be filled.

Blessed are the merciful: for they shall obtain mercy.

Blessed are the pure in heart: for they shall see God.

Blessed are the peacemakers: for they shall be called the children of God.

Blessed are they which are persecuted for righteousness' sake: for theirs is the kingdom of heaven.

Blessed are ye, when men shall revile you, and persecute you, and shall say all manner of evil against you falsely, for my sake.

Rejoice, and be exceeding glad: for great is your reward in heaven: for so persecuted they the prophets which were before you.

Other authorities on the paranormal disagree. Some cite his journal entries describing theurgy and the beginning of Esoteric Christianity, as well as references to the *Oration on the Dignity of Man* (*De hominis dignitate*, 1486), to make the case that the Spanish lord's ideas stood in opposition to Church teachings. *De hominis dignitate* is remembered as one of the more important public discourses made by Pico della Mirandola, whose writings shaped what would become the Reniassance.

What is not in dispute, however, is the obsession don Juan Jesús Díaz y Bahamonde had with the Seven Deadly Sins. In his journal, the first sentence on each page is the same:

Proverbs 18:9 states: "He also that is slothful in his work is brother to him that is a great waster."

Then that day's entry begins.

It was here, in front of this property, that don Juan Jesús Díaz y Bahamonde, according to his journal, lashed out against Sloth. And it is believed his incantations summoned Belphegor to this precise location.

Belphegor, in the Judeo-Christian tradition, is one of the princes of Hell. He deceives the lazy and rules over the deadly sin of Sloth. He is also, according to Jacques Collin de Plancy, Hell's ambassador to France. In 1818, Collin de Plancy published the *Dictionnaire infernal*, in which a profile of Belphegor emerges that influenced generations of commentators. It was a greatly popular book when it reached Mérida in the 1830s.

Belphegor is believed to summon rats to do his bidding in the world. Belphegor is said to dwell in this compound and to avail himself of an army of Demon Rats.

According to his journal entries, don Juan Jesús Díaz y Bahamonde thought the Maya were guilty of the deadly sin of Sloth. He believed life was designed to be hard work, arduous labor, serious business. In life, don Juan Jesús Díaz y Bahamonde believed, toil was necessary to save one's soul.

The Maya, in contrast, thought life was to be enjoyed. Theirs was a sensual outlook on living, one that embraced hedonism. The Spaniard had seen their rituals, where they cavorted almost naked in various stages of arousal and drunkenness. He had borne witness to the ceremonies in which incense and honeys, fragrances and oils were used to entice the senses. He was privy to the careless abandon in which they shared intimacies, glances, smiles, kisses, caresses, and embraces.

He saw all of this, but he saw no serious toil, no labor, no application of discipline to productive industry.

Spiritualists who have ventured to this place concur that Belphegor agreed with don Juan Jesús Díaz y Bahamonde that people in Yucatán were guilty of the deadly sin of Sloth. Belphegor concluded that the most appropriate

vengeance would be an army of tenné-colored (tan-orange-colored) rats with cerulean eyes, an army believed to live in a series of cenotes beneath García Gineres. The opening is a cavern located beneath the house located behind the walls of this compound.

Legend tells us this army of Demon Rats rises from their underground dwelling at night and races through Mérida in search of the slothful. They surround the guilty. They attack, devouring their flesh. They consume even the succulent marrow of the femurs. Then they return to this spot with that person's skull. It is delivered to Belphegor, who spits on the skull.

"I will deliver this soul to Hell," Belphegor says, smiling.

With that, the Demon Rats are dismissed for the night. Belphegor then takes that person's soul to Hell for eternal damnation.

133

In recent years the army of Demon Rats has been sighted in three locations.

They appear at the old railroad station, not far from Mejorada Park. Once there, one of the Demon Rats will assume the shape of a person and ask, "When is the next bullet train departing?"

The answer from whichever caretaker is on call is always the same. "There are no bullet trains."

The Demon Rat in the guise of a human replies: "Sloth!"

Then they vanish.

The other place is at the Siglo XXI Convention Center. One Demon Rat appearing in the shape of a human inquires, "When is the Palace of the Maya Civilization Museum to open?" He is answered that it is still under construction.

The Demon Rat in the guise of a human replies: "Sloth!"

Then they vanish.

The third place is the Governor's Palace on the Zócalo. The army rushes up the stairs and turns right. They assemble in front of the first door, where one rat takes the form of a human.

"Where is the Irresponsible Illiterate?" he asks.

He is answered: "The Irresponsible Illterate is on a trip somewhere. She is always on a trip somewhere."

The Demon Rat in the guise of a human replies: "Sloth!"

Then they vanish.

The army of Demon Rats is patient. They will wait for those guilty of the deadly sin of Sloth. They will devour their flesh and gnaw their bones. They will deliver the skull to Belphegor, who will then take that person's soul to Hell.

What is one to make of an army of Demon Rats unleashed in Mérida that hunts down, at the command of Belphegor, those guilty of Sloth?

To have one's flesh devoured by hordes of Demon Rats is a terrifying idea. To have one's soul delivered to Belphegor is a horrific thought.

And what became of don Juan Jesús Díaz y Bahamonde, the man who brought this haunting to Mérida?

Historical records are contradictory. There are some reports that he continued to Mexico City via Veracruz. Other records indicate that he returned to Madrid. His name surfaces in documents concerning the entourage of don Juan Carlos María Isidro de Borbón, Count of Montizón, remembered as the Carlist claimant to the throne of Spain between 1860 and 1868.

What is not in dispute, however, is that it is don Juan Jesús Díaz y Bahamonde who is held responsible for summoning Belphegor to Yucatán and unleashing an army of Demon Rats who pursue and devour those guilty of the deadly sin of Sloth.

Can you hear them? Have you seen their cerulean eyes peering out from their tenné-colored fur?

If you have, it might be the last thing you see.

It might be too late to do anything—anything *unslothful*—before the Demon Rats surround you and devour you alive.

Do you think your skull is shapely? How would it look with Belphegor's black spit dripping off it?

That is what awaits the slothful. This much is undeniable, even for those of us who are Irresponsible...and Illiterate.

Paranormal Activity: Ghost

Address: Calle 27, between Calle 16 and 18th Street, Colonia García Gineres

Classification: Malevolent

The Apparition of the
✠ Gentleman Killer ✠

A long the intersection of Avenida Reforma and Calle 35 one finds Quinta Alicia. This grand house was built in 1863 by Don Manuel Rodríguez Acosta, a renowned figure in the second half of nineteenth-century Yucatán.

There are other gracious homes along Calle 35 as one walks east toward Calle 60. Like Quinta Alicia, they reflect the taste and sensibilities of a time when, despite the turmoil of civil disturbances here and abroad, decorum endured and was valued.

People in Mérida at that time were taken by *La Mascotte* (*The Mascot*), an opéra comique by Edmond Audran, and *Chilpéric*, an opéra bouffe by Hervé. The 1888 waltz, "Sobre las Olas," or "Over the Waves," a song by Mexican composer Juventino Rosas still enjoyed at amusement parks the world over, was a sensation that circled the globe. Most famously, it is the song that now plays at the National Carousel in front of the Smithsonian in Washington, DC, today.

Not far from Quinta Alicia, in a residence since demolished, stood a private club where gentlemen gathered to drink, smoke, play parlor games, and talk business, science, and politics. One of these gentlemen, legend has it, had arrived in Mérida from Catalonia. The city he came from is in dispute, but it was not Barcelona. This man would slip into one of the private booths that were surrounded by lattice cages imported from London. He would indulge in Peking duck and roasted Yucatecan venison. One was topped with Russian caviar, the other was marinated in French champagne. The cigars came from Havana, and the scotch came from Scotland.

The pastimes were backgammon, cards, and chess. Gentlemen of the era in Mérida collected pocket watches, walking canes, glass flasks, and botanical specimens. Taxidermy featured prominently in their homes; and privately, daggers from across the ages were coveted and jealously guarded.

The Catalán immigrant, whose name is recorded as Roderic Moncada, enjoyed the debates that centered on the scientific inquiries of the day. The archaeological work at Uxmal by the audacious husband-and-wife team Augustus and Alice Le Plongeon enthralled the people of Mérida. For the first time there was serious scientific inquiry to establish the connections between ancient Mexico and ancient Egypt.

The Le Plongeons, with their state-of-the-art daguerreotype images, were documenting the vast Maya ceremonial center. When the Empress Carlotta arrived in Yucatán, they provided a private tour of Uxmal for her majesty. Roderic Moncada participated in the royal tour of the site and environs.

It is said that, as they left the Temple of the Phalli, Roderic Moncada stumbled and fell down a ravine. It is believed that Camazotz, the Maya bat god, appeared before him ,and that as the mortal gasped in fright, Camazotz flew into his mouth and possessed him.

Others in the party ran to his rescue, hearing his screams. They found him lying prostate near the opening of a cavern. They hurried him off to Hacienda Uxmal for his own well-being and also to remove him before the empress was made aware of the incident. The Le Plongeons wanted to spare her royal sensibilities from knowledge of this unfortunate event.

It is said that upon the arriving at Hacienda Uxmal, the Maya who gazed upon him were terrified. They claimed his eyes glowed with demonic possession; they made the sign of the cross and refused to remain in his presence. The Spaniards present didn't notice anything and dismissed the reactions as the hysterics of an irrational people.

Roderic Moncada recovered soon enough and was able to rejoin the royal entourage the following morning. He completed the tour without further incident.

When he returned to Mérida, however, things were different.

The Maya shunned him, making the sign of the cross when they saw him and excusing themselves from his presence. When they encountered him in public, the Maya would cross to the opposite side of the street. Spaniards and other Europeans were struck by his demeanor. He appeared later and later in the evening at the club and at social events and appeared withdrawn and distracted. Some witnesses report that he "appeared suddenly" out of nowhere.

Others were convinced he had the ability of bilocation—being in two distinct places at once. In the New World only Saint Martin de Porres is attributed with that miraculous gift.

What is certain, however, is that one day, after he left the club and walked home, he vanished.

Within months, reports of an apparition in this area began to surface. Out of nowhere a man would appear from the shadows. He was said to be dressed as Roderic Moncada favored and to carry a walking stick. He was said to approach pedestrians, most of whom grew fearful at the sight of this apparition.

There are reports that the apparition would approach a couple and ask for the time. When one of them answered, he would plunge a dagger murderously into the chest of the innocent. Reports indicate the other person would run, terrified, or collapse to the ground to assist the wounded companion.

By all accounts, the apparition then vanished into thin air.

There is consistency in the witness reports. The apparition, who speaks Spanish with a Catalán accent, always asks for the time. When he is answered, his reply is the same: "I congratulate you for knowing the hour of your death!"

He plunges a Scottish dirk, or dagger, into the victim's rib cage. He then vanishes.

Could it be that Camazotz possesses this man?

The Maya believe that Camazotz is exacting vengeance on the Europeans who have settled here, intent on slaying them one at a time before dragging their souls to Hell.

The apparition continues to be described as being capable of bilocation, not unlike Saint Martin de Porres who, in 1962, was canonized by Pope John XXIII. Saint Martin de Porres is the patron saint of mixed-race people and of all those who seek interracial harmony.

That, however, is not what the Maya believe of those who are under the influence of Camazotz.

You have been warned.

Should you find yourself strolling in the vicinity of Reforma and Calle 35 late at night or be walking along Calle 35 toward Calle 60 and a well-dressed gentleman appears, carry on. Do not stop. If he reaches out to you and asks for the time, do not answer.

He knows the time, and so do you.

Should you be foolish enough to answer this apparition's query, you will be rewarded for your troubles with the taking of your life.

The time, he asks?

It is time for your life to end.

Provided you answer, that is.

Paranormal Activity: **Spirit**

Address: **Calle 35, between Avenida Reforma and 60th Street, Centro**

Classification: **Malevolent**

The Ghosts of the Centenario

The Soul of the ✠ Madwoman ✠

hen it opened, the Hospital O'Horán was a state-of-the-art medical facility. It was second to none anywhere in the world.

Throughout Mexico it quickly acquired the reputation for treating inebriates, a synonym for alcoholics. The hospital also treated "lunacy" and "idiocy," familiar conditions at the time. A century later, in our time, "lunatics" and "idiots" are normally diagnosed as suffering from manic depression or bipolar affective disorder (BAD). No longer locked up, they can now be medicated.

That explains a great deal about the world in which we live today, doesn't it?

Located on Avenida Itzaes, between Calle 59 and 59-A Street, there is a modern facility behind the original hospital building.

It is that original building that is of interest to us here. In 1910, Henry Lane Wilson arrived in Mérida on his way to Mexico City, which was a familiar route during that time. (Travelers would sail to Havana, then continue to the Port of Progreso, journey to Mérida, continue to Campeche and then set sail to Veracruz.) He had been named United States ambassador to Mexico by President William Howard Taft. He traveled from Washington, DC, to Mérida before continuing on to Mexico City to take up his post.

There is a legend about a young woman who was part of Wilson's entourage and who was taken ill in Mérida. She claimed, inexplicably, that she could not continue to the capital. She believed that should she reach Mexico City, it would be end of her. She said she grew fearful of the plans for continuing the trip. This sudden attack came two days after she attended a dinner party hosted by a prominent family in town in honor of Henry Lane Wilson.

Wilson dismissed her illness as the consequence of the long journey from Washington and the tropical climate. Two doctors agreed, and she was taken to the Hospital O'Horán. They claimed she suffered from an extreme case of hysterics, more commonly known as conversion disorder. Now considered a form of neurosis, at the time it was seen as an ailment that attacked primarily women and was a result of their constitution, which was thought to be weaker than a man's.

The young woman insisted she was not mad. She claimed to know that she would be in danger if she reached Mexico City. She made wild allegations against Henry Lane Wilson and accused prominent members of Mérida's elite of conspiracy. She spoke of plots and schemes and of assassination. It all created quite a scandal. She was tied to her bed and sedated. The Americans were the first to call her a madwoman. The treating physicians at the Hospital O'Horán were more liberal in their diagnosis.

The American delegation discreetly sought to distance themselves from her. A local doctor was contracted to oversee her care. The delegation continued on their journey as planned without mentioning that she was being left behind.

In the weeks that followed, her primary-care physician claimed she represented a threat to public health. He cited "hysterical contagion," imitative behavior associated with hysteria. He did not elaborate on this diagnosis. She was restrained and isolated from any further contact with anyone else.

The Madwoman, as she was called, insisted that her sanity was intact. She insisted that "dark forces" were

descending on Mexico City.

She was sedated more heavily. She was further isolated from the medical staff.

When she claimed that the United States was conspiring with sinister elements to carry out political assassinations, she was diagnosed as insane, a diagnosis that permitted a more aggressive course of treatment. She was subjected to higher dosages of sedatives and psychiatric drugs.

In the course of her treatment, she suffered a reaction. After a subsequent episode, she died.

Within two years, and during Wilson's ambassadorship, there was a coup against Mexican President Francisco Madero. He was assassinated on February 21, 1913.

It is said that, late at night, the ghost of a woman is seen wandering the corridors of the Hospital O'Horán and repeating one word: *Assassin!*

Then she raises her index finger to her lips.

Is the ghost of this Madwoman real? Many in Mérida who have seen her swear she is as real as you or I, gentle reader.

"Assassin!" The ghost of the Madwoman whispers the word across the decades.

Who can believe such a delusional claim? One would have to be insane.

Or so claimed His Excellency Henry Lane Wilson.

Paranormal Activity: Ghost

Address: Avenida Itzaes, between Calle 59 and 59-A Street, Centro

Classification: Benevolent

The Spirit of the
✠ Remorseful Brother ✠

The former Juárez Penitentiary is one of the more haunted buildings in Mérida.

To date, there have been seven distinct paranormal presences identified roaming the halls, corridors, and cells of this former prison. Only three have been contacted by spiritualists in a definitive manner. Of these, only one's identity—and story—has been verified.

It is the spirit of a man imprisoned for the murder of his brother. He occupies the northeastern corner of the *Ex-Penitencería Juárez*. Enraged over his father's preference for the younger of two sons, this man murdered his younger sibling and was imprisoned.

The murderous rage of one child against another is as old as humanity. Genesis 4:1–8 teaches:

> And Adam knew Eve his wife; and she conceived, and bare Cain, and said, I have gotten a man from the LORD.
>
> And she again bare his brother Abel. And Abel was a keeper of sheep, but Cain was a tiller of the ground.
>
> And in the process of time it came to pass, that Cain brought of the fruit of the ground an offering unto the LORD.
>
> And Abel, he also brought of the firstlings of his flock and of the fat thereof. And the LORD had respect unto Abel and to his offering:
>
> But unto Cain and to his offering he had not respect. And Cain was very wroth, and his countenance fell.
>
> And the LORD said unto Cain, Why art thou wroth? and why is thy countenance fallen?

If thou doest well, shalt thou not be accepted? and if thou doest not well, sin lieth at the door. And unto thee shall be his desire, and thou shalt rule over him.

And Cain talked with Abel his brother: and it came to pass, when they were in the field, that Cain rose up against Abel his brother, and slew him.

In this haunting, a man had three children, a daughter who died in infancy and two sons. His wealth was diminished by the collapse of the henequen, or sisal, industry around the world in the early part of the twentieth century.

With the family fortune reduced, concerns grew about their future. In the face of such relative impoverishment, Javier Fajardo, as the spirit identified himself, grew worried about the size of his eventual inheritance. Prison records indicate several inmates with a similar name during the time in question. The spirit laments that his family estate became *arruinada*, or ruined. There is disagreement on this point because one spiritualist insists that the spirit is saying *Arrigunaga*, which is a surname.

This discrepancy among clairvoyants aside, there are other documented facts surrounding how Javier slew his brother Aurelio. He claims remorse for having done so, more for the manner in which he murdered his brother than for the punishment he received.

The spirit claims that he enticed his brother with the promise of inviting him to a dance hosted by the beautiful sisters María and Beatriz de Regil. The younger brother, excited about the prospect of attending a party in the company of these young ladies, was eager to impress. Javier suggested he take a bath with the castile soap their mother used on special occasion. While his brother was bathing Javier entered the bathroom, which boasted a porcelain bathtub of Edwardian proportions.

As Javier approached him, the younger man was distracted, talking about the sisters and which shirt to wear. The older brother reached for a wooden brush.

"Here," Javier reports saying, "you'll need this to scrub your back."

The young man reached for the brush his brother held aloft. Then Javier struck his brother on the side of the head with the wooden brush, and he struck again. He then knelt by the bathtub as he held his wounded brother underwater.

"I saw the bubbles rise from his mouth and nose as he struggled to breath," the spirit recalls. "I held him as he drowned, and the gash on the side of his skull bled."

The murderer ran out of the bathroom and out of the house.

Not until the next day did a maid enter the younger man's bathroom and discover the body.

The spirit communicates that his mother instantly knew what had happened. When she ran to the bathroom upon being informed, she held her son's partially submerged body in the bloodied bathwater. Her eyes were filled with tears as she cried out in anguish.

"I have lost all my children!" she cried to the maid. "My daughter to death, this one to murder, and the oldest son to the mark of Cain!" she said.

The father collapsed when told. Within two years, he would be dead.

It was the father, however, who notified the authorities of the murder of his younger son. Immediately afterward, he summoned his remaining child.

The spirit claims that his father asked, "Where is your brother?"

In that moment, he knew his father was aware of the truth.

The spirit, in life, replied nothing.

"I don't know why, but God has now taken everything from me," the father said. Then he pronounced: "You are no longer my son."

In life, Javier Fajardo languished in jail. When he was released, his father had long been dead. His mother forgave him, but she died within a year after he left the Juárez Penitentiary.

Ruined and without immediate family, he lived out the rest of his days as a recluse. The final thing he remembers of the world of the living is being administered last rites.

Then he opened his eyes...and found himself, a spirit, confined to the Ex-Penitenceria Juárez.

One clairvoyant reports that the spirit says, "I am condemned to wander the halls of this confinement."

Is this what you hear? Is this what he tells you? Is this a place of banishment?

Is Mérida a place of isolation?

Paranormal Activity: **Spirit**

Address: **Avenida Itzaes and Parque de la Paz, Centro**

Classification: **Benign**

✠ The Ghosts of the ✠ Dancing Pedophiles

I n terms of poetic justice, this is perhaps the most unusual haunting in Mérida. It is one that speaks of Purgatory, a reminder to the living of the price of sin.

For more than a century the Parque del Centenario—Centenary Park—has been a gathering place for families. Constructed to commemorate Mexico's centennial (1810–1910), the park was inaugurated by President Porfirio Díaz when he toured Mérida. It has remained a splendid place, a pastoral sight of life-affirming domestic tranquility where the people of Mérida gather to enjoy the tender pleasures of family life.

The fountain that stands at the entrance to the park has witnessed the sighting of the ghosts of two pedophiles who were murdered when their victims turned on them and smashed open their skulls.

The ghosts appear to levitate over the fountain. They are dancing. One is wearing a leotard and a pink tutu. He appears to be leaping, and his hands move in a theatrical circular motion. There is a clarinet sticking out of his rectum. He is said to be mouthing, "I'm a Dancer!" He plays the clarinet by farting.

The other ghost is seen as an obese man on all fours with a leash around his neck. He sports a dramatic leather hood that is shaped like a dog's face. It includes an elongated zip-front snout with breathing holes and attentive ears. A leather dog's tail, attached to a latex butt plug, protrudes from his rectum. He wears a dog tag that reads Papito Miguelito, meaning Daddy Mickey. He is said to jump through hoops as he runs circles around the first ghost who dances and leaps. The second ghost is said to mouth the expression, "Breed me like a bitch!"

What is one to make of this? Two ghosts, one leaping in dance and the other running in circles on all fours like a dog?

One psychic has noted that the two ghosts appear to be living out a scene from *The Garden of Earthly Delights* by Hieronymus Bosch. Recall that Hieronymus Bosch, the

151

Dutch artist, painted that triptych between 1490 and 1510. It hangs in the Prado Museum in Madrid and portrays the torments of damnation. The right panel of this triptych is a Hellscape. Considered by historians and art critics as warning of the perils of giving in to base desire, the work depicts scenes similar to this haunting. In the painting, several figures have musical instruments inserted in their rectums, and there are various depictions of bestiality.

Another psychic, who claims to have communicated with the two ghosts, says they were foreigners who lived in Mérida. She confides that they ran a sex-tourism enterprise, bringing tourists to Mérida to indulge in earthly perversions. She claims they were pedophiles who often secured victims from nearby towns.

Conkal is one of the villages from which boys were lured and brought to Mérida. Here they were sexually abused by these pedophiles and their paying visitors. She reports that the pedophiles' activities were exposed and that officers of the law located several of the youngsters who had been violated. She claims both men met ghastly deaths, murdered by the youngsters they had raped.

Their ghosts are said to appear at dawn, presumably because in life they never woke early, having spent the entire night in nefarious activities. Psychic investigators claim that the two, who in life were despicable, now languish in Purgatory.

These monsters who walked the earth are now confined to this fountain, as if the water beneath them could wash away their sins. They are imprisoned over a fountain of imprisonment, where they can no longer harm anyone.

Some say they have been condemned to haunt a place where they are surrounded by children but are no longer able to rape them.

It is one of the most terrifying and ghastly spectacles of all of Mérida's paranormal sightings.

How many places on Earth can boast a ghost who plays the clarinet shoved up his rectum by farting?

One ghost may be a dancer and the other a human-canine. But we all know in life they were human filth, and now both are the damned.

Paranormal Activity: Ghosts
Address: Avenida Itzaes and 59th Street, Centro
Classification: Malevolent

final Notes

The Virgin of
✠ Guadalupe ✠

Reported Apparitions of the Virgin

𝔄 mid all this paranormal activity reported throughout Mérida, we may be inclined to wonder: What of the Virgin of Guadalupe?

Has she been seen in Mérida?

On May 25, 1754, Pope Benedict XIV declared Our Lady of Guadalupe to be the patron saint of New Spain. With the papal brief *Non Est Equidem*, issued in 1754, the Vatican approved litrugical texts for the Holy Mass and the Breviary in her honor. In 1910 Pope Pius X proclaimed her patron of Latin America. Greater honors followed: In 1945 Pope Pius XII declared her Queen of Mexico and Empress of the Americas. The following year, the pope recognized her as Patroness of the Americas. In 1961 Pope John XXIII proclaimed her the Mother of the Americas. In 2002, Pope John Paul II canonized Juan Diego, a indigenous (Aztec) Christian to whom she first appeared on December 9, 1531, on a hill in the Tepeyac desert, on the outskirts of Mexico City. In 2002 the celebrations for Saint Juan Diego Cuauhtlatoatzin (December 9) and Our Lady of Guadalupe (December 12) entered the the liturgical calendar.

It is not surprising to know that the Virgin of Guadalupe has appeared on various occasions to the faithful throughout Mexico and around the world.

In Mérida there are five locations where she is reported to have appeared. In the course of these investigations into paranormal activities, two of these locations have been confirmed. They are both in Santiago.

The Virgin of Guadalupe is said to appear suspended before the *espadaña*, or belfry, of the Church of Santiago the Apostle. She faces the church and is believed to be praying for the souls of the four infants whose bodies were thrown on the roof for carrion to devour. She is also said to appear in the interior courtyard of the building located on Calle 59, numbered 572, between Calle 72 and 74 Street. She faces the fountain, as if praying to someone on the other side. She is believed to be comforting the soul of La Llorona, the young mother who murdered her three children.

There is no official statement from ecclesiastical authorities on the reported apparitions of the Virgin of Guadalupe in Mérida.

Investigating the
✠ Paranormal ✠

A Comment on Methodology

This book represents three years of research into paranormal sightings in Mérida. More than 300 incidents of paranormal cases have been reported to our office for investigation. Those for which reliable information has been confirmed are included here.

To understand the process used, consider the circumstances surrounding "The Anguish of the Spirit of the *Titanic* Mourner." To verify this story, apart from witness accounts of the broken plates appearing on the kitchen floor in the house in question and the conclusion of a psychic who has visited the residence, basic questions had to be answered. How many people aboard the *Titanic* were bound for Mexico or Cuba? (Havana was a gateway to Yucatán in 1912.) Of these people, how many survived the disaster at sea? Which lifeboats did they board? Are there records of telegrams arriving in Mérida from survivors?

It turns out there were seven passengers bound for Mexico or Cuba. Two, both bound for Mexico City, traveled first class. Both drowned. Of the five bound for Havana, one traveled first class. He perished. The remaining four passengers, traveling in second class, survived the ordeal. Two were men and two were women, the sisters Florentina and Asunción Durán Moré. Records indicate the sisters were aboard Lifeboat 12 when they were rescued. There is no documentation of any telegrams *arriving* in Mérida from these women, but there is a record of a telegram being sent to Mérida *from* Havana by Asunción Durán Moré. The image included here is the death certificate for Florentina Durán Moré, who died in Havana on October 1, 1959. This begins to flesh out the details in the story, substantiating the principal facts of the haunting of the house on Calle 64, #451, between Calle 53 and 55th Street.

The same process was repeated for every other account included in this collection. In this manner, as many details as possible have been ascertained for each story included here.

        ❧✠❧

All biblical quotations are from the Kings James Bible.

        ❧✠❧

Finally, the author is grateful to Christine Valentine, one of New York's most gifted editors, who patiently reviewed the manuscript and offered insightful commentary.

CPSIA information can be obtained
at www.ICGtesting.com
Printed in the USA
FFHW010925071218
49722138-54147FF